ALSO BY BARBARA WOODHOUSE

NO BAD DOGS: The Woodhouse Way
WALKIES: Dog Training and Care
          the Woodhouse Way

BARBARA'S

WORLD OF

HORSES AND PONIES

Their Care and Training the Woodhouse Way

BARBARA WOODHOUSE

Summit Books
New York

GRATEFUL ACKNOWLEDGMENT IS MADE TO THE FOLLOWING FOR
THEIR PHOTOGRAPHS:

PETER GREENLAND—PP. 11, 44, 54, 74, 75, 79, 106; AMERICAN
SADDLEBRED HORSE ASSOCIATION—PP. 2, 31, 110; AMERICAN QUARTER HORSE
ASSOCIATION—PP. 14, 82, 83, 104; WELSH PONY SOCIETY OF AMERICA—
PP. 20, 69; RED PONY RANCH—P. 90; THE JOCKEY CLUB—P. 111; APPALOOSA
HORSE CLUB—P. 114; ALL OTHER PHOTOGRAPHS BY DR. MICHAEL
WOODHOUSE.

PUBLISHED BY SUMMIT BOOKS
A DIVISION OF SIMON & SCHUSTER, INC.
SIMON & SCHUSTER BUILDING
1230 AVENUE OF THE AMERICAS
NEW YORK, NEW YORK 10020
SUMMIT BOOKS AND COLOPHON ARE TRADEMARKS OF
SIMON & SCHUSTER, INC.
FIRST PUBLISHED IN GREAT BRITAIN IN 1954 BY BARBARA WOODHOUSE AS
BOOK OF PONIES. ALSO PUBLISHED IN GREAT BRITAIN IN 1981 BY
KESTRAL BOOKS, PENGUIN BOOKS LTD.
DESIGNED BY EVE METZ
MANUFACTURED IN THE UNITED STATES OF AMERICA

10   9   8   7   6   5   4   3   2   1

LIBRARY OF CONGRESS CATALOGING IN PUBLICATION DATA

WOODHOUSE, BARBARA, DATE.
   HORSES AND PONIES.

   PREVIOUSLY PUBLISHED AS: BOOK OF PONIES. 1954.
   1. PONIES. 2. HORSES. I. TITLE.
SF315.W8 1984   636.1'0887   83-20372
ISBN 0-46141-9

Contents

Juno, the author's Great Dane, offers a piece of bread to Sixpence.

1·Horses
and Ponies

In this book I hope youngsters of all ages will find all they want to know about keeping a pony. Many will not even own a pony, but will still want to learn everything about it. To know everything about ponies makes riding or helping to look after other people's ponies so much more fun.

If I had a fairy godmother and she granted me one wish, it would be that everyone who ever rode a pony, or came into contact with one, or only just loved ponies would know the same happiness I have had from these delightful animals all my life. In this book I have done my best to pass on everything I know so that those who would like to learn may do so.

As I watch our modern youngsters and their ponies, I know they are missing a lot of pleasure in the way some of them ride and look after their mounts. Is it because the old-fashioned groom, who taught us when we were young to grip with our knees and sit up straight, has disappeared? Is it because in his place are neat young men and women, who never learned the good old ways and who allow the riders to clutter up their horses and ponies with every sort of contraption to achieve control, without teaching the child (or adult, for that matter) that a dropped noseband is the hallmark of bad hands? Any pony whose mouth has to be kept shut and controlled by force is in my opinion not only a disgrace to its breaker and rider but a sign that the old words "beautiful hands" are becoming a thing of the past.

I am going to write an easily read book in the hope that the pendulum will swing the other way, and that in the future children and grown-ups may read this book and want to find out for themselves the true joy of being one with their horse or pony—a pony being a small horse that stands no more than 14.2 hands high.

How many pictures, I wonder, of people who really spend their lives in the saddle would show them with short stirrups and reins held awkwardly in two hands? Very few. Look at the police horse and its rider. No short stirrups for him. Watch a Western film on television or at the movies. Do you ever see those horsemen, even though they are only actors, riding with their knees in the awkward position you see far too many riders take up today? No, the people whose lives and careers depend on long hours in the saddle know that comfort for horse and rider increases the staying powers of both. I learned to ride the hard way as soon as I could toddle. The hard way was to find out for myself what kept me in the saddle and what didn't; the hard way was to be poor and not be able to buy expensive saddles and stirrup leathers; the hard way taught me that if I rode depending on my leathers for support and safety, and I made an error of balance over a jump or my pony shied, my stirrup leather invariably broke, and I landed uncomfortably and possibly dangerously on the ground. This made me realize that to rely on the leathers was very foolish, and that true balance

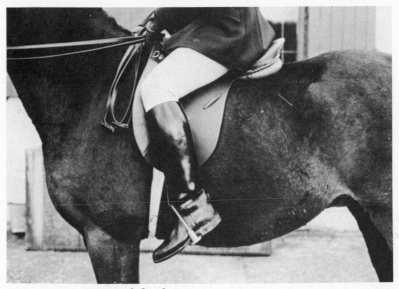

Incorrect position of the foot.

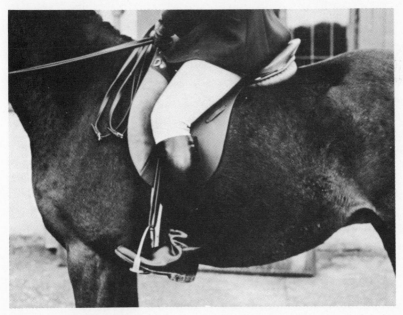

Correct position of the foot.

and comfort were attained only by the ball of the foot lightly balancing on the stirrup. I learned that in this manner, with the stirrup-iron turned inward toward the instep, there was far less danger of its coming off my foot. How often today you see the toe pressed down over the end of the stirrup or shot home right into the iron! I always say a little prayer that the rider won't fall off and get his or her foot trapped in the iron and thus be dragged and injured.

Why is this all wrong? With the heel dropped, the calf muscle is tightened and naturally holds fast to the flap of the saddle without any effort of gripping. How many experienced riders grip their saddles? I think very few. It is too tiring. With the toe nicely balanced in the iron, and a sensibly long stirrup leather, the rider's whole position is comfortable, allowing her to sit naturally in the seat of the saddle, not perched up on her pelvis half on the pommel of the saddle—which is what I see far too often.

I spent many years in Argentina, where I lived in the saddle for long hours. All my work and pleasure was with horses. If my readers could see the Indians of South America riding their quick, alert little cow ponies with nothing more than a single rein, and a blanket for a saddle, they would see perfection of ease and movement. Whatever the pony does, whether it shies or makes a sudden leap over a snake, the rider does not for a second leave his position. No danger, in this partnership, of horse and rider's parting company; no swerve sends the Indian into the grass on his nose, for he lives not only *with* his pony but *on* his pony for the greatest part of both their lives.

When I lived down there, I had to ride sixty miles to do my shopping. I could not have done so had riding been the effort it must be to some of the riders of today. For one thing, the reins were held with a minimum of contact between the bit and the sensitive bars of the pony's mouth. Down there, the pony was trained on a piece of rawhide which never touched the part of the mouth that the bit would eventually touch. The bit for me was a pelham; for the Argentines a curb with one rein only, so that the pony made no mistake, should correction be necessary, as to who was master.

You never see horses pulling in that part of the world; their jaws would break if they fought against some of the fierce bits they are ridden in. Is it cruel? In my opinion, no! Because the *neck* is used for guiding the horse—not the bit, as in this country. All horses are neck-reined on a completely loose rein held lightly (although naturally there are cruel riders in all countries) in one hand; the cowhands of Argentina and other countries need their free hand for the lasso. Their ponies must also be handy. They must stop in their own length. No struggling, fighting animal that pulled on his hands when he wished to stop would be of the slightest good to a cowboy chasing a runaway steer, or bringing in a herd of sheep, well known for stupidity. No! When you live on your horse you have to tire it as little as possible, and yourself as well.

Why is it that Argentine polo ponies fetch vast sums of money outside their own country? Though many of them are only cow ponies, costing very little in their native land, they bring enormous prices when exported elsewhere. The answer is that the polo player can concentrate on the game without bothering about what his mount is going to do. They are accustomed to barging into cattle and pushing them around. They are toughened by having been driven into their work and had their muscles hardened from an early age. Never do we see a cow pony pull up on its forehand to send a jolt through the rider's head. No! It slides its back feet up to its front ones and applies the brakes with everything it possesses. Why is this? These ponies know only too well the punishment they would get on the severe bit if they didn't; and in addition, they have already had good practice from rounding up the cattle. Make no mistake, the ponies love riding around the herd. The "old hands"

An American Quarter Horse trained to slide its hind feet up to its front ones and apply the brakes.

can twist and turn on their own account faster than the rider can guide them. The cowboy of Argentina knows very well that it is easier to let his horse's mouth alone than to attempt to guide by it. All he does is bend his body with the pony and give the help it needs.

The speed of these tough little ponies is amazing. There again, I am sorry to say, they have learned to be fast to save themselves pain, for the riders wear sharp-pointed spurs, and don't hesitate to use them. Yet never have I seen blood on their flanks, as I have seen at show-jumping contests in other countries. Which shows that it isn't the sharpest spurs that always do the most damage.

How much do we want to copy these and other riders of the range? A lot, I think. Naturally, I do not support cruel bits and spurs; but in the following chapters I am going to tell you what I think could be used to advantage to recapture the ease and beauty of riding horses and ponies, which in my opinion we are in danger of losing.

I have no intention of going into competition work or show work. I am not in the least interested in winning ribbons for ponies or horses any more than I am for dogs. Nor do I really enjoy seeing little children on expensive ponies cavorting around a show ring. I love seeing children on children's real ponies, riding them as if they were part and parcel of them, and it is to those children, and any grownups who are humble enough to want to read my book, that I shall talk in these pages.

The author with a pony that has been living rough.

2·Choosing a Pony

MONEY AND THE CONDITIONS under which the animal is going to be kept naturally govern the type of horse or pony that my reader will want.

If the pony has to live rough, out all winter in an orchard or field, the fine-boned, highly bred pony would be out of place. It must be in a warm stable, blanketed and clipped, and looking so beautiful that the owner's every free moment is spent admiring its beauty over the stable door. It is the same with the Arab, although if some toughening blood has been crossed into their veins these breeds live out well. I myself have an Arab-Welsh cross, with a mat-thick coat that no rain could penetrate. If I am ever foolish enough to pity her in vile weather and bring her in, she fumes and frets to go out again. She just turns her back to the icy wind and rain and scrapes away the snow with her foot to find her own food. Even when hay is put out for her, she seldom eats it. It is a type of crossbred pony I strongly recommend for any child with not much money to spend.

Small and medium ponies for the smaller children, with larger ponies for the bigger ones, are hard to beat. But once the child reaches about fourteen years old, I think a 15-hand horse (except for certain show classes) or even something bigger is essential, as the child can gain much knowledge and joy from its different length of stride. The large ponies usually have better shoulders, and the older child can benefit from gaining control of something with more character than the average child's pony.

Children should, of course, start with an older, gentle pony which has proved itself to be safe as a mount, to gain confidence. But far too many children carry on far too long with this type of pony. They never learn to be on their guard, as they should be with a more spirited mount. Half the fun of riding is, year after year, to get ponies or horses with new tricks or idiosyncrasies to conquer. Not until you have eaten mud many, many times will you, to my way of thinking, be a good rider ready to tackle nearly anything with four legs and enjoy it.

I always turn around to watch if I see a child riding gracefully with the pony's head gently bent to the will of the rider's reins and thoughts, a proud look on its face and spring in its step. Yet it is possible to get this from practically any pony if you know how.

Conformation counts a lot, we know. But I have often bought horses with the wrong conformation and turned them into glorious smooth rides.

I like the short neck and high head carriage of the Arab. I don't enjoy the long neck of many Thoroughbreds. If you have a pony "well coupled up" with a nice short back, good quarters and a reasonably high head carriage, you can always train it to be very handy. That is the type of pony I would choose for myself or my child.

I once bought a five-year-old pony out of a farm cart, a dun, which had looked nothing in harness, but by the time I had given it a changed head carriage and taught it to jump, it was the ideal mount.

I never worry about a horse's mouth. All mouths, in my opinion, can be changed with a changed head carriage, and by teaching the animal to answer to your wishes by telepathy and voice.

Far, far too many ponies are ridden like bicycles with four speeds—walk, trot, canter and gallop—without being taught that these things can be achieved without going through the slowest to reach the fastest. How many ponies break instantly and easily from a standstill into a canter without much preliminary kicking and thumping with a crop? Not half as many as I would like to see. Yet with the aid of thighs, calves, hands and voice, not to mention thoughts, this can be the smoothest of actions.

Let's leave, then, the question of what sort of pony to have to the future purchaser. The main thing is to get a pony without vices. One that shies or rears, or is unsafe in traffic, or bites or kicks in the stable, should never be contemplated. There are specialists who do nothing else but re-breaking, but this type of pony or horse should never be bought for a child, and very rarely for the ordinary adult rider. The mount of this type is no fun at all, and riding should be fun and a relaxation. You can't relax on a pony with vices.

Having a pony on trial, if it can be arranged, is a good idea, for an unfit pony will often show no vice at all, yet when ridden and fed it may develop all sorts of vices. Buy a pretty pony, as far as it is possible to do so; a child is always encouraged to take care of the pony really well if it is pleasing to look at. Not all children love animals enough to pour out their love on the not-so-beautiful ones.

Above all, buy a pony that will stand up to the work that is required of it, as there is nothing so heartbreaking as choosing a pony, spending months schooling it to perfection and then finding its legs or wind won't stand up to the pace.

I know that many people employ a veterinarian to look over a pony before purchasing it. That is all very well if it is an expensive pony; but few veterinarians could give a clean

A Cob-type Welsh Pony stallion.

certificate to an old pony, even though it may be quite suitable for a child to ride. So I am going to outline a few things to look for, both important and not so important.

FEET

A pony without feet—good feet—is a useless proposition, and a vast number of horses and ponies suffer with their feet. An attack of "fever in the foot"—or "laminitis," to give its correct name—may have put the pony's front feet in very bad shape. You can usually spot this without even looking at the feet by the "tied-in" action of the pony. By this I mean that to ease itself, the pony has considerably shortened its stride; it doesn't like the banging its feet get in an extended trot. Therefore, beware of a pony that takes little short steps. Actually, if you mount the pony and try to post to this trot, your back will ache very quickly. In the past, unscrupulous horse dealers would file off the lines on the outside of the hoof, which are a clear indication that the pony has at some time had "founder" or laminitis. The other indication is the shape of the foot: it is often slightly dished. Maybe if the attack has been mild and the foot is growing out strong and well again, it could be worth the risk of buying the pony, provided it is going to work mostly on soft ground. Clever shoeing can do much to remedy this condition. The overgrown toe typical of this disease can be kept pared well back, and the sensitive sole of the foot can be helped with a protective piece of leather or a plastic pad. But unless the pony has little work to do, I personally would steer well clear of any signs of this disease, for once it has attacked there is a predisposition to recurrence.

There is also a serious and dangerous disease of the foot called "navicular" which is a form of arthritis, affecting the navicular bone in the foot (*navicula* means "little boat"). It gets progressively worse and is without hope of cure. The main thing for my readers to look for is the pointing, in a resting position, of one, or sometimes both, front feet. In the old days, aging carriage horses could be seen resting one foot in the forward position. Ponies are very apt to have this trouble and should never be purchased if it is suspected. Always get a veterinarian's advice if you have the slightest suspicion of this. A good idea is to examine the foot, and if the shoes are very worn away at the front toes, beware. The animal may only need reshoeing, but it may have a much more serious defect.

Personally, I always ask a blacksmith about feet. I'd rather pay a blacksmith with years of experience a reasonable sum to look at the feet of an intended purchase than all the veterinarians in the world, much as I respect the profession.

LEGS

Here we tackle a very difficult subject, for few children's ponies or older horses have what I call "clean legs," without blemish. In fact, I doubt if I would buy one without a few lumps and bumps, or I might imagine it had done very little work, and instead of being unsound it might have a few tricks to overcome.

"Wind-puffs" are the most usual deformity to be found in any pony that has done a lot of work. Sometimes these soft lumps on one or both sides of the tendon sheath just above the fetlock are only just visible; but I have seen them as big as eggs.

Usually they cause no trouble, and in some cases I have seen them in breeding stock that have never done a day's work. When they start developing on a young pony they can be immensely helped by cold bandages, or a poultice spread over the swellings to dry at night. Shoes with raised heels also help. But I have never had much trouble from this type of wind-puff, and I would advise the purchaser of an otherwise good pony to ignore them. Their unsightliness is their worst feature.

"Splints" are bony enlargements that appear most commonly on the inside or outside of the cannonbone of the front legs. Most ponies and horses get them before they reach six years old. They may be large or small. What matters most is where they are located, and how you can recognize them. Stand in front of the pony and look at the big bone down the front of its leg; then run your hand lightly

The author pointing to a wind-puff.

down it. If your hands are sensitive, you will be able to feel your fingers go over a sort of rise or lump and then go on smoothly again. That is a splint, which is a calcium deposit. Naturally, if it is well developed you will be able to see it without this test. I always remember when I went to buy my daughter a rocking horse and the salesclerk looked amazedly at me as, without thinking, I ran my hands down its front legs. I was so used to buying and selling horses that I did it automatically. When you have handled as many horses, good, bad and indifferent, as I have, these things become second nature, and the fingers become sensitive to the slightest problem. But I do not expect my reader to be so skilled. All I want to do is point out the general faults.

Well, the next thing to inspect is the position of the splint. Normally, splints don't interfere at all with the horse's working powers. I think all my horses have had them. But should the splint be large and halfway down the cannon-bone (on the inside of the leg), it may be struck by the shoe on the other front foot, if the pony is a bad mover, thus causing lameness; or if too far back, it may involve the tendon. Normally, however, a splint may be disregarded.

TENDONS

A sprain of the tendon running down the back of the leg is a bad defect. To check for this, face the side of the horse and run your touching thumb and forefinger lightly down the back of the cannonbone. With a really sound pony, the finger and thumb will stay in contact. But should there be some injury, new or old, that will not be possible, as there will be puffiness from inflammation or scarring. The seriousness of this cannot be assessed in this book—it is up to a veterinarian; but should there be pronounced swelling down the back of your pony's legs between the back of the knee and the fetlock, beware, and seek expert advice. Prolonged lameness can be caused by sprained tendons, which are called bowed tendons.

Most of the troubles I have mentioned have been in the front legs; splints, wind-puffs and tendon troubles can of course occur in the back legs as well, which should be examined in the same way. Most lameness seems, however, to occur in the front legs.

WIND

I think that deciding that a pony is sound in wind is probably a veterinarian's job. As the pony is cantered and galloped past him or her, the veterinarian should be able to hear even the faintest "whistle." A pony with this whistle is called a "roarer," and it means that the animal is unsound. But for a child's pony all we need is a *reasonably* sound pony, and a slight whistle can be ignored. Unless you are paying a fairly big price for a pony, a very slight noise in no way impairs its usefulness.

The "heaves," a condition caused either by a respiratory disease or by an allergy, is often a progressive trouble, which may worsen quickly or may take years of hard work to grow troublesome. A "heavie," or pony with this condition, can be spotted by the double heave of its flank as it breathes.

The various unsoundnesses to be found in horse and pony are numerous, and I don't propose to deal with them in any more detail here. If you intend to pay a lot for your pony, it always makes sense to get a good veterinarian to examine it.

The author with Star and his new mistress.

3·Care of the Pony

YOUR PONY HAS ARRIVED, and I feel sure that before its arrival you have done everything to ensure its comfort. A few children have grooms to look after their ponies, and have little else to do but appear nicely dressed and ride their mounts. But this chapter is not concerned with them, for even though some readers may think them lucky, I don't. Half the fun of owning any animal is to look after it yourself, thus learning all about it. I know it is hard work if it lives in the stable, but it is worthwhile work; and by having to look after your pony, you build up a bond of true love and friendship that you could never achieve through only riding it.

First, I am going to deal with the pony that is stabled in winter.

If the pony is going to be clipped, it must have a warm, draftproof stable, with plenty of light and ventilation.

The feed bowl should be such that it can be washed out, and the hay net or rack should be at a convenient height for the pony. Never have a hayrack so high that the pony has to stretch its neck upward to reach its food, or one day it will get hayseeds in its eyes or ears. For you see, when you clip out a pony properly, you clip the protective hair away from the inside of the ear. A hayseed in the eye can cause profuse inflammation and even blindness.

There should be a ring in the wall to which you can tie your pony for grooming. I never like the ring in the manger, for all the dust from the pony's coat inevitably goes into it, which means more work cleaning it out.

The implements needed for thorough cleaning and grooming of the pony are one dandy brush; one body brush; one currycomb; one water brush and one small shoe brush

Grooming equipment: top row from left: tail bandage, mane comb, hoof pick, water brush; second row from left: dandy brush, body brush, currycomb, hoof oil; bottom row: leg bandages.

for oiling the hooves before going out, to make the pony look its best. You will need a hoof pick for removing the dung that has gotten pressed into the hooves overnight; a steel mane-and-tail comb and two or three cheap, ordinary combs for pulling the mane and tail; a tail bandage and if your pony hasn't the best of legs, four leg bandages and a roll of cotton batting. This list shows that for many birthdays and Christmases to come you will need presents to use on the pony.

When stabled, the pony must have exercise once a day. This may mean getting up early and taking it out before you go to school; or if you haven't time for that, it may mean fifteen minutes a day on the lungeing rein in the paddock. This is only second best to a ride, as it soon bores both pony and owner.

If you haven't time for this, don't keep your pony in a stable, for you cannot expect a pony to stand in a stable during the week and then have a strenuous weekend. To get a pony fit, regular exercise is essential, even though it need not be fast exercise. An unfit pony stumbles, and is in danger of injuring its wind.

FEEDING

First of all let us consider what the essential factors in a pony's diet are. There are three main essentials: proteins, carbohydrates and fat. The proteins form the flesh, the carbohydrates are the starch for energy and the fats are for heat. Besides these, of course, there are water, salts and vitamins. The diet of all animals has two aspects: the maintenance diet, on which a horse not working or doing only very light work can exist, and the production diet, on which the horse draws for its working energy. Good grass can provide both in summer, but in winter, hay is the maintenance diet and oats the production ration. Every animal has its basic daily maintenance ration—which for a horse is 20 pounds of hay, but which varies in quantity with the size of the animal. You wouldn't expect a Shetland pony to consume this amount! For a pony the usual diet, if it is working hard, is 10 pounds of good hay, 8 pounds of good oats and 2 pounds of bran per day.

Some people like to make up the feed with chaff, to keep the pony from bolting its oats and giving itself indigestion or even colic. Never buy new oats—always old oats, and be sure they are well crushed. Always weigh the ration, unless you are a very old hand at the game—different bags of oats weigh quite differently—and if you give, say, half a bucket a day one week from one sack, next week, with a different crushing, the oats may weigh entirely differently. Always feed this meal dry unless the oats are dusty, in which case they can be very slightly dampened. If this is the case, leave out the bran and increase the oats, for wet bran acts as a laxative, which the pony does not need for working.

The hay should be a clover mixture if possible, not meadow hay, Very green or leafy hay again acts as a purgative and may cause the pony to be very loose, in which state it is obviously not good to ride.

Water should always be left for the pony—nice clean water, and plenty of it. A pony that always has plenty of water never drinks too much. In fact, I always left the water bucket quite near the manger, and my lovely Arab mare Wendy, whom I brought from Argentina with me, used to dip her nose into it after every mouthful of oats to wash it! But she never overdrank.

GROOMING

To keep a pony healthy while stabled, you *must* give it a daily grooming. Any child who grooms a pony only when she feels like it should not have a pony. The pores of

An American Saddlebred in beautiful condition and freshly groomed.

the skin must be kept clean and unclogged, and the daily massage achieved by a good grooming tones up the muscles and helps to make the pony fit.

If the pony is clipped, the dandy brush will be used only for its mane and tail—it is too harsh for a pony's sensitive skin. So many ponies are made vicious by harsh grooming with the wrong brush. When grooming the belly, take special care not to do it with too much vigor, as it is a very ticklish part of the anatomy, and the pony can quickly learn to kick if you are not considerate about this.

Always start at the head and work toward the tail. Groom with a firm circular motion at first, constantly cleaning your brush on the currycomb and banging out the dust from the currycomb by knocking it on its side on the floor. Next, brush away the dust that has been raised out of the coat in the circular motion by dampening the brush slightly—or if you have two brushes, keep one as the water brush; then finish off with a nice, soft yellow duster. Wash the tail by immersing it in a bucket of warm water and soapsuds; rinse and shake out well. Apply your tail bandage starting at the top and working downward for about twelve inches and then up again. A good groom gets the bandage on so that it finishes right at the top of the tail and the knot is tied on the top outside part of it. Turn the loose ends in underneath the tapes. Neatness counts for a lot in stable management.

CLEANING THE STABLE

Few children may at first believe there is a great art in the cleaning of a stable.

Straw should always be used. Always give a pony a nice, deep bed; it is no cheaper to give too little straw, as the pony will probably mill around and mess it all up. Always pile up the straw around the outside edges of the stable. Not only does this ensure that the stable is not drafty when the pony lies down, but it prevents the pony from injuring itself in moving around. It also means there is straw available for replacement on the center of the floor if you haven't time in the early morning to bring fresh straw.

You will need a four-pronged dung fork for easy working. Start with your wheelbarrow at the stable door—having first tied up the pony to prevent a sudden exodus out the door over the wheelbarrow; then remove all the solid dung you can see by picking it up on the fork and turning the fork over and shaking off the dung as you reach the wheelbarrow. That saves straw, and at the price it is today, it is a big consideration. Next, pile up all the clean straw around the edges of the stable, and give the floor a thorough brushing with a good stable broom. I am going to presume you have a good floor with a safe foothold for the pony. If it is a floor of square bricks, wet manure gets between the bricks, and the quickest way to clean it is to get the hose and hose it down. Then replace the straw, throwing it well into the air as you spread it so as to let it fall at all angles, which makes a comfortable and safe bedding.

Lastly, rinse out the water bucket and fill it to the brim with clean water, not pond water.

If you are riding that morning, put some oil on your pony's hooves. You can get any amount of waste motor oil from any garage, and a tin of oil lasts a long time.

SHOEING

Be sure to examine your pony's feet every day for signs of loose shoes, or nails that are coming through the front of the hoof, or signs that the pony needs its shoes removed. This last problem is indicated when the sides of the shoes are working inward from the outside wall of the hoof, where they should rest, and pressing on the sole of the hoof. This can cause a severe corn by its pressure, and should never be allowed to happen. The pony should be shod once a month if doing heavy road work, or at least have the shoes removed and the feet trimmed once a month. Some ponies are harder on shoes than others. And some wear out their shoes at different rates on different feet, so always examine all four feet.

LICE

Always make sure your pony is free of lice. A pony can sometimes pick them up while grazing with other stock. Should you find that your pony is infested, bathe it with flea-and-tick shampoo, making sure to soak the entire coat and rubbing it well into the bottom of the hair. The base of the mane and tail and ears are the most common places for these insects. Be careful not to get any shampoo into the ears or eyes. Always get someone to hold a hand over the eyes of the pony as you wash its head.

WASHING

If you are going to show in summer, to get your pony's coat looking really lovely, give it a thorough washing with soft soap; then walk the pony on a halter until it is dry.

When the weather is very hot and your pony comes in covered in dry sweat, or even when damp, you can throw a bucket or two of water over it and scrape it dry with a scraper which can be bought at a saddler's. Polo ponies are always washed after every chukker, or period, and it keeps them beautifully clean. They soon get used to the cold water, and when scraped and rubbed down with a chamois leather they get a marvelous shine on their coats. This must be done only in hot weather unless the pony is to be kept moving until dry.

CLIPPING

Unless you own an electric clipper, the best thing to do is take your pony to the local riding school, or to friends who have a machine, and ask them if they will be so kind as to clip it for you. You would be surprised at how much skill is involved, for if you clip the pony unevenly it looks awful and the coat takes weeks to grow out. You should never clip a pony until it has fully grown its winter coat, which is about October. I used to clip mine at the end of October; before that you won't get such good results. If the pony is going to live in a stable, you want to clip it all over the first time, legs and all, as it would look very rough with the thick hair left on its legs; but the second time it is clipped, which is usually about eight weeks later, leave the hair on the legs to protect them against brambles and thorns.

If your pony is going to live out of doors and you are going to work it hard, give it a trace clip only—a partial clip beginning under the pony's throat and continuing down along its chest and under its belly. This keeps it from getting too hot and muddy, yet gives it enough protection from the elements.

Sometimes ponies are very nervous about being clipped, and when their heads are being done you may have to use a twitch, which is a piece of string on a stick twisted around the upper lip to keep the pony still. This is cruel and should be used only as a very last resort. I have usually found that if you breathe gently up the pony's nose before you start, thus showing that you are friendly, and use endearing words and stroke it gently as you work, you give the pony confidence in you. Occasionally, a sharp word brings a hysterical pony to its senses.

Always clip against the flow of hair, and leave a saddle mark to protect the back. Never leave a clipped pony standing about in cold weather or in a draft. And never clip a pony that has a cold or is in any way unwell. Use thick

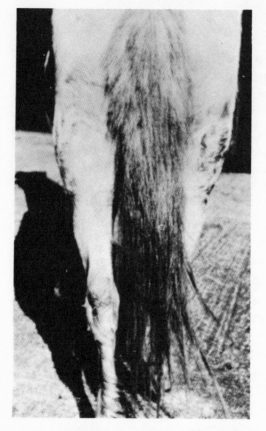

An unpulled tail.

blankets to keep it warm; the number required will depend on the condition of your stable. You can always tell whether a pony is warm by feeling its ears. If the ears are cold, so is the pony, and vice versa.

The clippers should be very sharp, and constantly oiled to prevent them from getting hot and causing discomfort to the pony.

PULLING THE MANE AND TAIL

If you want your pony to look really handsome, it is almost essential to tidy up the mane and tail, unless it is very well bred and hasn't too much hair. Then you can keep the mane and tail long and well combed and brushed. But even then there must come a time when both mane and tail need attention to keep them looking really nice.

There is no reason at all why any girl with reasonably strong fingers shouldn't learn this art. Years ago, when I was dealing in horses, I could instantly tell when a horse had passed through a certain dealer's hands no matter what the present owner said, because of the way its tail was pulled. A work of art and patience if ever there was one! And people have kindly said the same about horses that have passed through my hands; but then, I owe that to the teaching of an old-fashioned groom whose gnarled hands almost caressed the manes and tails, and tidied them up without resentment on the part of the horse. This is absolutely essential when you're pulling a tail, or you may get some broken bones from a restless horse that kicks in resentment.

The first thing to do is protect the ring finger of your left hand by covering the middle joint with adhesive tape, for it

Adhesive tape protects your ring finger while you're pulling the tail.

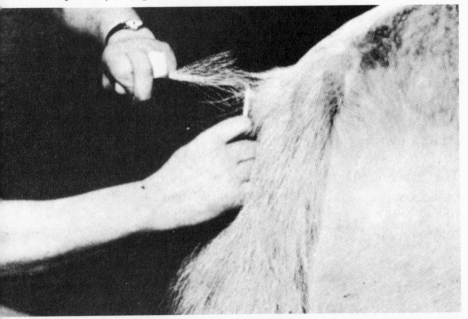

is this joint that really does the work. I have torn the skin off mine hundreds of times in my life (and the result can be quite painful), although I was usually too busy looking at my handiwork to bother much.

Next, get a fairly fine-toothed comb; you can buy one quite cheaply at any variety store or drugstore. You need one that is handbag size; a bigger one would not do. Tie up the pony, and talk to it soothingly as you approach its tail.

Comb the tail thoroughly so that all the hairs are hanging straight down. Look at the tail and decide exactly how thin you want it to be. Remember, once the hair is pulled it takes weeks to grow long again. If the pony is to be kept in and the tail bandaged, you can pull it quite "tight" into the bone, because the hair will always grow nicely if kept bandaged at night. But if the pony lives outdoors and you only want to improve its looks and thin out a too-heavy tail, you should pull it mostly from underneath; otherwise it will grow again and strongly resemble a chimney brush. Never, under any circumstances whatsoever, *cut* the tail (except for trimming the bottom); it will look nice for a few days and then it will grow outward and be tough and bristly. Heaven help the person who has to pull a tail that has once or twice been cut!

Always pull a very small quantity of hair at a time, and take it equally from both sides; if you take big chunks of hair you will leave a bare patch. Next, holding the hair to be pulled in your left hand, comb the loose ends upward against the hair until your comb has pressed them almost back to the bone. Then, with the comb as near the base of the hair as you can get, press down hard on the hair, and with a quick jerk with the third finger of your left hand, pull sharply downward with comb and left hand simultaneously. You will probably be surprised how easily the hair comes out. Few ponies object; some slightly itchy ones think it lovely and will squirm to get you to do it where it itches most.

Pulling the tail.

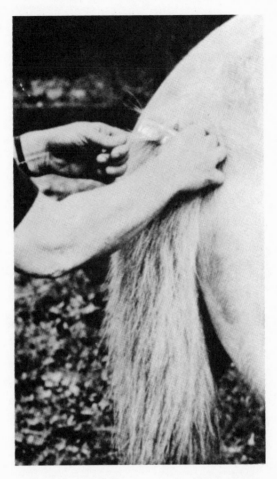

Every owner must decide for herself to what extent she wants the tail pulled. But for a stabled pony it should be neatly pulled from as close to the dock (tailbone) as possible to within about sixteen inches of the end of the tail. It will taper nicely if done proficiently.

Next, the tail should be cut straight across at the bottom. This should never be done when the pony is standing with its tail hanging straight down. Preferably, get a friend to hold the tail out in the natural carriage assumed when the pony is being ridden, and then cut the tail while it is held

A *semi-pulled tail*.

in that position to about three to four inches below the hock. If the tail is too thick to look nice, pull some hair from the center with your steel comb; a cheap comb would break on the bushy end of the tail. Dampen and bandage the tail after pulling.

To bandage a tail, start the bandage at the top of the tail, leaving the end sticking out crosswise. Holding the tail

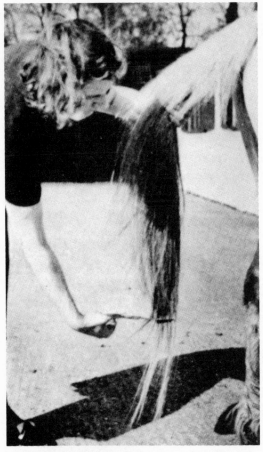

Cutting the tail to the correct length.

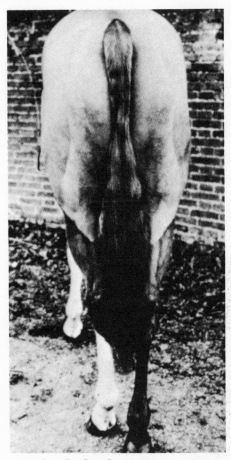

A finished tail.

away from the body with your left hand, bandage firmly down to the end of where you have pulled it short, then up again in a crisscross fashion. Before the last one or two folds, tuck in the flap you left out and bandage over it. That will keep it firmly in place. Tie a square knot and tuck the loose ends in under themselves. The knot must be outside at the top of the tail. If you don't succeed in getting it right at first, keep trying until you do. Rome wasn't built in a day. You will be the envy of all your friends if you can pull a tail nicely.

If the tail bandage keeps falling off, get a tail guard which is fixed to the surcingle and overcomes this trouble. Be very careful not to have the tapes of the tail bandage too tight. They can cause severe pain, and it is difficult for the wounds to heal.

The mane is pulled on the same principle as the tail, except that you have to decide what length you want, and must always pull the hairs that are longer than that length. It always amazes me what a perfectly straight line one gets by this method. Always pull the hair from underneath— never from the top, or you will get loose short ends, and the mane will look a mess. I always used to pull my horses' manes to about eight inches. But if you have an Arab, you may like to leave its mane long and keep it just the right length by occasionally pulling the too-long ends. In this

The mane before pulling.

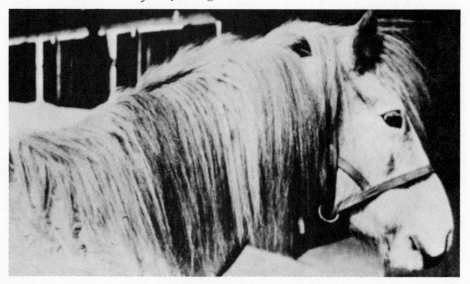

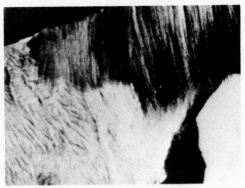

Correct way to hold the comb and the hair.

A half-pulled mane.

case, keep dampening the mane and combing it firmly down into place every day.

PLAITING

Now that you have pulled your pony's mane, you want it to look extra handsome when you go hunting, or to a gymkhana or a Pony Club meet. So the next thing to learn is to plait the mane nicely. Six plaits were considered correct, and in my young days if I did more than that I was frowned on by those who knew better. The choice is yours. Before plaiting you want to get the clipper, or a sharp pair of scissors, and cut short the hair that goes underneath the bridle on the poll behind the ears, so that it doesn't pull when the pony is bridled up. Also the hair that goes up over the withers in front of the saddle, for that can also be painful for the pony if it catches under the tree of the saddle.

Now you will need a bucket of water, a dandy brush, a big darning needle and strong black thread.

Brush your pony's mane thoroughly and comb it; then dampen it with water. Divide the hair into equal bunches, and start plaiting, tightly and evenly. Again, practice makes perfect; I'd be ashamed to go out on some of the ponies whose manes I see badly plaited. Start as near the base of the hair as you possibly can and make the plait very even. When you reach the end, pick up your threaded darning needle. Use a long thread with a knot at the end. Push it through the hair at the end of the plait and then wind it tightly around the bottom, about half an inch up.

With the needle and thread still in the plait, bend the plait double underneath itself, and the end of the plait should then touch the neck underneath the mane. Pass the needle firmly through both thicknesses of the plait, and put several stitches up and down the double thickness until the

A finished mane pulled and plaited.

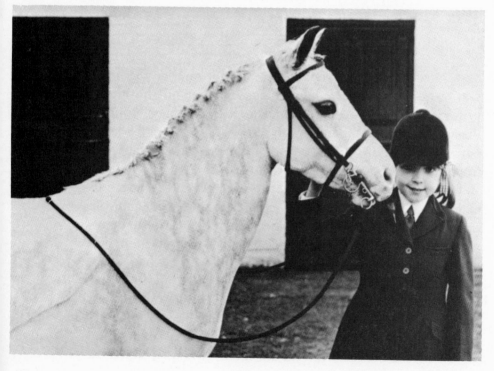

44

plait is securely fastened; then tie a knot and cut off the end of the thread. Repeat this with all plaits.

Never keep the plaits in for more than one day, or you will spoil the hair very quickly. Snip the stitches out with a pair of sharp nail scissors, being very careful not to cut the hair. Dampen the hair and it will soon lie naturally flat again.

If you are too busy to look after a pony's mane properly, it is better to "hog," or "roach," it, which means taking it right off with the clippers. In Argentina the natives clip their ponies' manes with shears, leaving more on in the middle than at the two ends. This gives the ponies "more neck," and might well be copied here on those "ewe-necked" ponies which look so horrid with their "upside-down" necks that go down where they should go up.

POINTS TO REMEMBER
ON CARE OF THE PONY

Feed your pony at least one hour before riding.

Give it very little hay if you are riding or hunting that morning.

Give the bulk of the hay at night.

Always check the dung of a pony. It should be firm, dark brown and rounded. If it is loose or bright yellowish-brown, the pony is unwell, and should not be ridden. If this condition continues, call the veterinarian.

If the pony comes in hot from riding, do not put its blanket directly onto its back. Put on a fishnet blanket, or "cooler," with a loose surcingle and leave it on until the pony is dry. Then it can be blanketed in the usual way. The surcingle should be put on tight enough to keep the blanket in place, but you should be able to fit in two fingers side by side between it and the pony's back.

Never ride a pony in leg bandages unless absolutely necessary. They can be dangerous to the pony, causing obstruction of circulation, or they can cause an accident if they come loose. If your pony needs them for protection during transport or because of a problem with its legs, always apply the bandages over cotton batting as a protective foundation, or you may cause injury to the tendons. Run them right down to the coronet at night, but only to the fetlock for working in. Far too many youngsters today put them on for looks' sake. A well-schooled pony seldom needs them for protection.

HEALTH

Every owner of a pony should know the signs of good and bad health. Good health is signified by a healthy appetite; a bright, clear eye; an alert expression; a shining coat; a clear nose and firm dung. Any discharge from eyes or nose is wrong; it is very often the first sign of a "cold," which is an infection of horses similar to our flu, or "strangles," which is a dangerous bacteriological infection. Strangles can be detected in an early stage if the glands under the chin and those behind the cheekbones are enlarged. When the pony has had a bad attack of strangles, the gland under the chin often bursts, exuding masses of pus. Occasionally there are outbreaks of strangles in a district, and if this is so in your area, you would be well advised to consult your veterinarian about giving your pony a protective vaccine. If a pony has suffered from strangles its wind can very easily be damaged, aside from the fact that the animal is out of action for many weeks.

The feet of a pony should always be ice cold. Naturally, they are warm when the pony comes in from exercise; but any heat in the foot after the animal has been stabled for some hours is a grave warning of trouble. Coughing or

46

The author with a healthy, well-cared-for pony.

sneezing should also be a warning; it might signal an infection. Dusty food, though, also may cause a pony to cough.

Shivering is always a danger signal. Take the pony's temperature at once, by placing the thermometer bulb well into the rectum. The normal temperature of a pony is within a range of 99° to 101°F—slightly higher in a young pony. Anything above that means a fever, and the veterinarian should be called.

Always examine a pony that scratches or rubs itself a lot. It may have a skin disease. Some ponies suffer from what is known as "sweet itch" or "Queensland itch," which is really an allergic itchiness caused by small biting gnats. The disease is usually seen in the warmer seasons, since that is when the gnats are more prevalent. A pony may rub its tail and mane quite bare in its effort to alleviate the irritation, and a veterinarian should be consulted.

Any other red or bare patches, especially if they smell, should have expert attention. Ringworm is particularly nasty, as human beings can catch it. So if you see any round, bare, itchy patches, don't touch them without rubber gloves until you have consulted the veterinarian.

A girl who loves a pony and lives with it as much as possible is soon able to detect if anything is wrong. Sometimes it may only be that the pony is not so willing to go fast, or sweats more than usual. If these symptoms occur, bring the pony home at once, and keep it warm in case something is developing.

4·Tack

"TACK" IS THE WORD USED in horsy circles for all the leather equipment you will need for your pony. It doesn't need to be an armory of saddles and bridles and bits. Years ago, grooms had an awful time cleaning steel bits by burnishing them with sandpaper and goodness knows what. Today we are lucky. Chromium plate saves us all this drudgery; a wash in warm water and a rub with metal polish will give us in a few minutes what the old ostlers and grooms used to take hours to do.

In my experience, only one bit is necessary for nearly every type of horse or pony: a rubber pelham, with varying lengths of sidepiece. I know that thousands of children and riders use a snaffle, so that there is only one rein to hold. But when you acquire the good hands I hope to teach you to have, you will need only one rein anyway—and that should be on the curb of the bit. Until you do acquire those hands, you should use a joiner from the snaffle ring to the curb ring of this pelham. This again gives you only one rein. Learn, by all means, when you are very young, on a snaffle, as the beginner's pony probably won't have a mouth at all anyway, and I think most riding-school horses can be saved from torture by inexperienced riders by having snaffles in their mouths.

In this book, we are going to be "pelham fans" and thus give the pony the maximum freedom from heavy hands and pinching bits. If you want to ride the way I, and other people who almost live on horseback in other countries, ride, you will need a simple bridle, with an ordinary noseband purely for looks, and a narrow, light pair of reins that are the longest you can buy. For with me, you are not going to drive your pony *into* its bit—you are going to have a pony beau-

A properly bridled pony.

tifully collected *behind* its bit, waiting to obey your every command, by voice, aid and thought. If you have a dropped noseband, go and bury it in the nearest quicksand and never look back. If you aren't prepared to do that, I advise you to do the same with this book, for it won't help you any further.

Having found a nice bridle—preferably a really beautifully kept secondhand one that was made when leather was leather—you must now get a saddle that fits your pony. There are many different types of saddles. If you intend to be a show jumper, you may prefer one with forward flaps that encourage you to shorten your stirrups and perch up on the pony's neck. But in this book, I am going to recommend an ordinary straight-flapped saddle that fits well down behind the pony's withers, leaving enough space when the girths are done up to allow passage of air along its spine and no rubbing to cause a sore back.

A horse fitted with a dropped noseband and a running martingale.

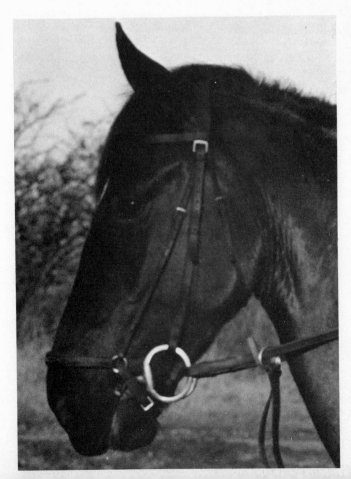

The width of the tree of the saddle is all-important; a fat pony will need a wide tree, and a narrow, high-withered pony a narrower tree. Personally, I would take the pony along to the saddler and let him fit the saddle. With his expert knowledge he can pad it up or take padding out as required.

The right choice of girth is essential, for if the girth rubs the pony, it will be out of use for many weeks with a "girth gall" or "girth pinch," names that are given to a horrid sore lump which appears after the skin has been pinched by the girth behind the pony's elbow. I always prefer a leather

Plenty of room between the tree of the saddle and the pony's withers.

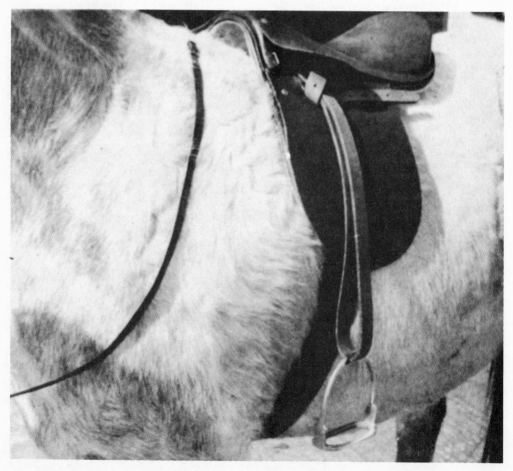

The right amount of clearance between the saddle and the pony's backbone.

girth that is lined with flannel soaked in neat's-foot oil, which, if you keep the girth clean, makes certain it never gets hard. If, however, your pony has a badly shaped shoulder, the girth is inclined to push itself forward under the front leg and cause a gall. If this is the case, use a narrow crossed-over type of girth known as the "Balding girth" which absolutely prevents this from happening. I always used this type of girth on my polo ponies, as very often after coming over from Argentina they were not hardened up.

Leather must always be sponged clean after use; this must *never* be left until the next day. Immediately after it is sponged clean, apply a good glycerine saddle soap and hang it up to dry. Polish it with a soft cloth the next day.

If, however, you can't afford a leather girth, an ordinary webbing one will do, provided it is not too wide; and above all, keep it clean by brushing it thoroughly when the mud has dried on it and occasionally washing it in soapsuds. It is never safe to go out on a girth with only one buckle and strap. If you want only a single girth, ask the saddler for one with two buckles, then if by any mischance one strap breaks you have another to keep the saddle in place.

To hold the saddle in the right position, the two straps should be fastened to the two outside straps—never to the two forward straps unless the pony is very "herring-gutted," which means it does not have much middle and the saddle tends to slip back. And by preference, if your pony is so built it is safer to fix the saddle forward with a breast strap to avoid the dangers of its slipping back.

Always put the straps up higher on the saddle on the "off" side, which is opposite the mounting side, so that there are plenty of holes left on your near side for you to adjust the tightness of the girth when you are out for your ride. Many ponies blow themselves up when you are girthing them; then when you get started, you find your girths hanging in

Tightening the girth after mounting.

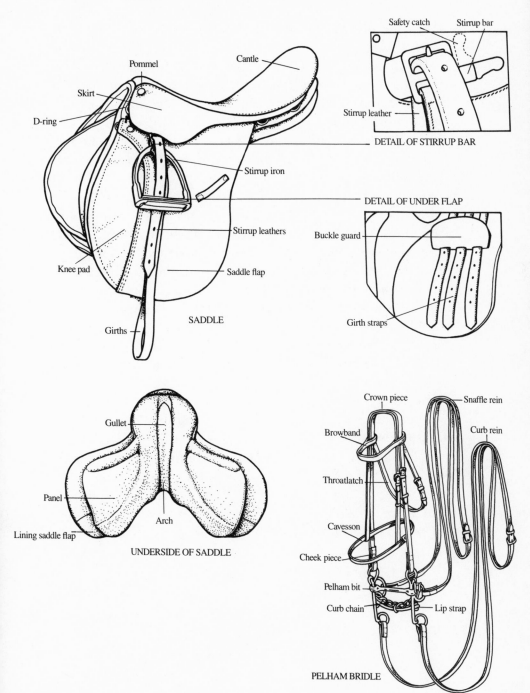

Safety catch Stirrup bar

Stirrup leather

DETAIL OF STIRRUP BAR

Pommel Cantle

Skirt

D-ring

Stirrup iron

Stirrup leathers

Knee pad

Saddle flap

Girths

SADDLE

DETAIL OF UNDER FLAP

Buckle guard

Girth straps

Gullet

Panel

Arch

Lining saddle flap

UNDERSIDE OF SADDLE

Crown piece Snaffle rein

Browband Curb rein

Throatlatch

Cavesson

Cheek piece

Pelham bit

Curb chain Lip strap

PELHAM BRIDLE

loops. So always check your girth a short while after you start.

When you're girthing up, it helps considerably to make the pony stretch itself by putting its front feet forward. Teach it to do this by touching its front legs with your foot and letting them drop into a more forward position. The girth should be only tight enough to allow two fingers placed side by side to get between it and the pony's body. Too tight a girth causes a gall.

If your pony has a wrong head carriage and is inclined to throw its head up when you pull on the reins, unless you can rebreak it and give it the correct head carriage you would be wise to ride in a standing martingale. This consists of a neck band and a strap through which the girth is threaded at one end and the noseband under the chin at the other. It should be only tight enough to prevent the pony's head from getting unmanageably high. Too tight a martingale tires the pony. A better solution would be to rebreak the pony using the Gloster noseband, which I will discuss later in this book.

The curb chain should apply pressure to the pony's lower jaw only when the curb is pulled half tight. When it is not being pulled and the pony is ridden on a lightly held rein with only light contact between bit and rein, the chain should hang free from the jaw. Remember, the curb chain is a punishment, and you don't wish to punish your ponies unless they are doing wrong. On the other hand, if the pony is a puller, the chain must be tight to teach that pulling hurts.

5·The Young Pony

So far I have assumed you have a well-behaved pony, and I have simply been teaching you the rudiments of care and management.

Now I am going to assume you have bought an unbroken pony of between three and four years, and want to train it your way to be the perfect mount.

Years ago, I used to break the wild horses of the pampas in Argentina for a big cattle ranch, or *estancia*. I broke them the way I was taught by an Indian—by breathing up their noses in the horses' own greeting; then all I had to do was show them what I wanted, and the horses were safe to ride anywhere within twenty-four hours.

I wonder whether many people know the value of the exchange of breath between horse and human achieved by gently breathing up each other's nose? I use it when a horse is frightened. I use it when I want a horse to put its entire trust in me, and it has never let me down.

Nonbelievers have watched me and called it magic, but it isn't magic, and what I do is achieved not only through the breathing-up-the-nostril trick: it is a combination of touch, tone of voice and telepathy which I use with all animals. The touch of one's fingers soothingly caressing backward and forward under the mane pleases a horse or pony so much that it will move its mouth and tongue in unison with the movements of your hand. Always watch a pony's mouth —it is the key to happiness and contentment or can signal nervousness and fear. A pony that is frightened opens its mouth sidewise, and one that is content lolls its tongue out of the side of its mouth. Wearing a dropped noseband prevents all use of the mouth to convey to its master or mistress whether a pony is happy in its bit or not—and therefore, again, it is not something ever to be used. The breathing-up-the-nose trick is an initial greeting—not to be repeated so often that the pony is bored. You don't keep shaking hands with people you know. You don't keep breathing up the nose of a broken-in pony. Ponies do it to each other when they meet for the first time; they don't do it again. I do it with a tame or broken-in pony only to calm it if it is anxious.

The tone of voice you use is equally important after the first meeting is over. I find that a soft up-and-down singsong voice makes a pony close its eyes in contentment. I've even had a formerly wild and difficult pony gently push its nose under my arm to get closer to me, as if the warmth comforted it. Far too few people talk to their ponies these days. The use of body aids and voice, not spurs and a hard, unyielding grip on the reins, is what should be cultivated.

Having achieved friendship by breathing up your pony's nose the first time you meet, make that friendship lifelong. Understand your pony's feelings, they are much like your

The breathing greeting.

Notice the horse's tongue moving to show its pleasure as the author gives the breathing greeting.

own. Ponies and horses are very sensitive to human feelings. If you are bad-tempered and irritable, your pony will pick it up. Happiness flows through the reins from your hands, and your tone of voice conveys your mood. Silence is not always golden with a pony.

I shall assume the young pony you wish to break is not a complete stranger to you. Perhaps you have bred it, or perhaps it has been grazing in your paddock. Which means that it has not been cruelly handled, as the Argentine ponies are when they are separated from their mothers, or come in for branding. I feel sure my reader will have taught the pony to take tidbits—of which sugar is by far the best for bribing it to be obedient, and for forging an understanding.

Some ponies haven't the faintest idea what sugar is and just won't eat it. I think it is important to *teach* a young pony to enjoy sugar. I suggest you get some granulated sugar and see if the pony will lick it off your hand. If not, rub some on its lips, or open the mouth with one finger in the side of its mouth and pop some onto its tongue. It will try to spit it out, but soon rather likes the taste and sucks it up instead. Daily offer it sugar in this way; then one day put on a halter and, holding the pony in one hand, pop a piece of lump sugar into the side of the mouth, if possible getting it between the back teeth. But don't get bitten by accident. In this way the pony is more than likely to chew the sugar even if it is only trying to get rid of it, and the taste soon makes it remember that it liked the same taste with soft sugar. In a very short space of time it is crunching up as much as you like to give it. That is the first step in breaking a pony—*bribery*.

I am also going to assume the youngster has been led around on a halter from an early age, as most foals are in England. If this is not the case, you will have to enclose the pony somewhere, and approach it very gently. Slowly, step by step, go up to it and after patting its neck and scratching under its mane, let the halter drop over its neck and hang down. Then change your hand position to underneath its

A youngster accustomed to a halter receives the breathing greeting.

neck, catching hold of the end of the rope. Tie it in a firm knot. This rope should be at least six feet long, as one cannot hold a pulling pony on a short rope, Next, very, very gently show the pony the halter and slip it on. Should the pony take fright and jump away, you can hold it by the halter, rather than the rope, as the halter will not tear your hands as the rope end will.

If you think you cannot hold the pony, never attempt to do this training yourself. Get a strong person to help you, as the pony must never escape or break the rope by which it is held. Once the pony has a halter on, it must be tied to a tree on a strong rope. From then on, it must learn that to "sit back" is useless; if possible, in fact, it should be made to *try* to sit back once or twice, just to convince it that you and the rope are master.

I always flapped sacks all over the ponies I was breaking. At first they were a bit frightened and always sat back once or twice, but soon they learned I wasn't going to hurt them, and grew calm. I advise you to do the same.

Now we will return to the pony that has learned it must be led without trying to run away or break away, and that has always received kind treatment from its owners.

Many people will tell you that the best way to train a pony is to lunge it on a long rein daily until it gets perfectly used to being controlled by this rein, and to carrying a saddle on its back. I disagree entirely. I have always felt that the first introduction to riding is terrifying for a young horse. It is chased by the human being and made to run away from him, although we know part of the training is to make it stand still and be approached and made much of. But I maintain that there is no need for this fearsome introduction to being ridden and driven. It is far better, to my way of thinking, to do everything lovingly, in close contact with the pony you eventually hope to ride.

My way is to take the pony into a box stall—a big one, if possible—and tie it up, being sure to have masses of straw on the ground to prevent slipping if the pony becomes frightened.

Then feed and pet the pony for a few days, and just walk it about. Throw your arms over it constantly, and lean as much as possible on its back, throwing one arm over its back and one arm under its chest. Pat its tummy. Pick up its feet. Brush its coat and mane. Put sacks on its back—empty at first and then filled with hay. Let these sacks fall off repeatedly from either side of the pony. It will be nervous at first, but the tone of your voice, warm, encouraging and loving, will soon reassure it. Eventually let the sack fall off over the pony's tail, and flap its legs with it gently. Give the pony sugar every time you let the sack drop. It will soon be looking for the sugar as a matter of course.

Now undo the rope that holds the pony, and walk gently forward holding the leading rope in one hand and the sack on its back with the other. If you have spent enough time putting it on and letting it drop off, all the pony will be looking for will be sugar. It will pay no attention to the sack.

Next put on a very light saddle using the method described on page 77, and attach the girth and pull it up very loosely; never attempt to tighten it at first. Walk the pony around, tightening the girth a hole at a time until the saddle is firmly held but the girth is not tight enough to be safe for riding. At this stage, leave the pony for at least an hour to walk about freely in the stable with the saddle on. If possible, use a felt saddle, with no tree to break if the pony rolls. I have never had a tree broken this way, even if the pony has rolled, but it is possible. So beg or borrow a very old saddle if you can. You might be able to buy one for a small amount at a saddler's.

The next step is to put a bridle on your pony and to mouth it, for it is this that will make or mar the animal for the rest of its life. And make no mistake: once a pony has a really bad mouth, it is a difficult thing to cure. But I will deal with that later.

First, place your saddle on the pony as usual. Next, get a bridle with a pair of strong reins. The bit, for our purpose, should be a straight-bar rubber pelham with short side-pieces. This type of bit is made in various widths. You must get one the right size for your pony, one that won't pinch the sides of its mouth. Here again your saddler will help you to choose the right fit.

Now bridle up the pony with the simple bridle I described in the previous chapter. I will explain the proper method of inserting the bit in the following chapter. Take

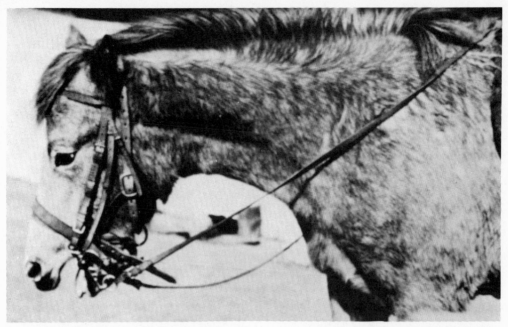

An unbroken pony mouthing itself.

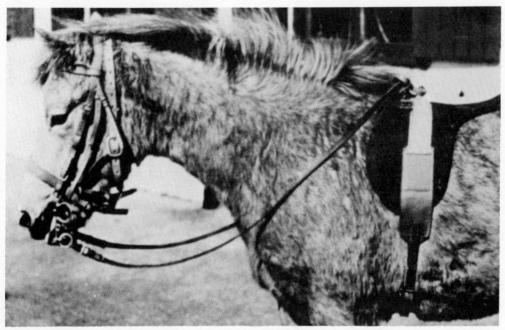

An unbroken pony bending to the rein after fifteen minutes of bitting for the first time.

the reins and attach them to the curb ring of the bit, but leave off the curb chain. Now run them back to the saddle and fix them to the bar, the part that normally holds the leathers. They should be loose, no attempt being made at first to get the pony's head into the position it will eventually be expected to have. The pony will chew and slobber at the mouth. Pay no attention. You should be far more worried if it doesn't chew and slobber, for in the old groom's words, "You must have a nice wet mouth to make a light one." In chewing the bit, the pony is "mouthing" itself. It is learning to tolerate this thing in its mouth and learning how to be comfortable with it in. It is learning that opening its mouth won't get it free from the bit, and thus it will learn to keep it shut. It is this mouthing that will keep the pony from needing that abomination of all abominations, the dropped noseband.

Once the pony is comfortably walking around its stable or standing still with its saddle and bridle on, let it do this for an hour a day for a few days. Then put on a halter over the bridle and take the pony out into a small paddock and walk around with it. If you are energetic, trot with it if it will trot; if it won't, you will have to get a friend to help the pony on from behind by waving her arms or touching it with a light twig, keeping far enough away from the animal's heels to prevent any risk of being kicked.

Now attach stirrup leathers and irons and let the pony walk around once more with them flapping around on the saddle. Flap them over its sides yourself, and talk soothingly as you do so.

Now get your hard riding hat on; take the pony out to your field, or if possible a straw-filled yard, and tie it up. Get a box or log and place it beside the pony. Have its saddle and bridle on, and a halter over the bridle with a rope attached, and tie up the pony with this. Gather up the reins in one hand, stand on the box and lean over the pony as far as you can, putting more and more weight on its back, until your feet are off the ground and all your weight is on the pony. Wave your arms around, and later your legs. Give the pony sugar, and do this a dozen times. When it doesn't bother the pony at all, slowly raise your right leg over its back, and there you are sitting on its back while it is still tied up. Even if it suddenly bucked, you would only slide off, as your feet should not be in the irons yet.

Next, slide off each side separately. When the pony ignores this exercise, use your irons to mount it. Turn its head to the right and left with the reins to get it used to your hands' holding them.

Next, if possible, get the help of a friend to lead the pony at a walking pace with you on its back, turning in circles. At this stage it is vital that you start to teach the pony what you want by your voice as well as your legs and seat. I always use the words "Walk on" for starting off, "Wee trot" for the trot and "Canter." When I wish to stop, I say "Shhh." You will be surprised how quickly the pony will learn to recognize these sounds, and eventually will obey them with hardly any other aid.

When you urge your pony on, most of the work is done with your thighs and buttocks. Heels aren't nearly so important.

Every time you say "Shhh" to stop your pony, you must gently pull the mouth, but the person who is leading the pony for you must stop it on the halter. The aim is to teach the pony obedience before the mouth is ever used. Once it knows the meaning of words coupled with aids, its mouth will be so lightly used that it won't fight at all. When the pony stops, it must immediately be made to "back," for without teaching your pony to back easily you will never get a balanced ride. If it won't back, pull gently on the bit, and your friend must push very hard on the noseband of the halter. Give the pony sugar even if it takes only one step back. Always use the words "Walk back."

The next step is a trot, and if the pony has shown no signs

of objecting to you being on its back, I see no reason for it to do anything terrible when you urge it into a trot. Provided you are in a strawed yard or soft enclosure, little can happen to you. In any case, you would not be attempting to break your own pony without being a reasonably good rider.

At this stage, put the pony back into the stable and once more attach its bridle to the saddle with the pelham in its mouth, but this time put on the curb chain. Let it be tight when the pony's head is held straight down, but as soon as the neck bends slightly, the chain should be free of the chin. Let the pony walk around for one hour a day in the stable and eventually in the small paddock or yard with its head tied back to its saddle as directed. Thus the pony is mouthing itself, and learning to bend easily and kindly to the touch of the bit and curb chain. Provided you have good hands, this is all the mouthing necessary. Should the pony attempt to get its tongue over the bit, tie a piece of string in the middle of the bit, bring the ends out of the sides of its mouth and knot them on the front of the noseband. It cannot then get its tongue over and will soon forget the silly habit. A pony with its tongue over the bit is not easily controlled.

The next stage of breaking in must be in circles. It is essential to get the pony supple and willing to obey your every command. I want you to teach your pony to neck-rein, as polo ponies do, and for this I suggest you let the pony wear a halter as well as a bridle, and attach reins to the sides of the halter. You will then have two reins in each hand. When you want the pony to turn to the right, pull the rein of the halter hard to the right and lay the rein attached to the bit on the left side of the pony's neck. Keep pressure of any sort off the bit. If you turn right and left like this for some time, you can soon do it by neck reining alone. Then, after you take off the halter, the pony does it easily with the lightest of holds on the bit.

A young rider on his Welsh Pony.

If the pony is difficult to turn, use the lightest of twigs or lightly press your crop, on the shoulder opposite the way you wish to turn: for example, a tap on the left shoulder if you wish to turn right, and vice versa.

This helps the pony to turn without hollowing itself by turning its head around too much. This is where neck reining is so far superior to pulling, as the head stays in line comfortably with the body, and the pony is far more likely to change legs easily. This leads to the next stage, which is to get the pony on the correct leg. In going in a right-hand circle, the right foreleg should strike off to the lead; otherwise the pony is either on the wrong leg or "disunited," and both are extremely uncomfortable.

Disunited means that the front and hind legs on the same side of the pony are not working in unison as they should be. If this happens, the pony should be checked and started off again. To get a pony to lead correctly with the right leg on a right-hand circle and a left leg on a left-hand circle, make it canter in very small circles. If it continues to lead with the wrong leg, increase its speed and narrow its circle. Use your thigh to help it lead off; watch when the correct leg is forward and attempt to urge it forward quickly at the right moment, applying your heel vigorously into the ribs on the opposite side of the horse, thereby driving it into the circle. Some people turn the head slightly to the left when driving the pony with their legs, seat and body into a right circle; others turn the head the way it is going. Experience will teach you which way is better.

I am not going into this finer art of schooling. There are plenty of books to consult, and as you become a good rider you will find out for yourself what aids help most to get a quick response. One thing I think is most important is to get a pony cantering from a standstill and to stay in a controlled, balanced canter on a loose rein for as long as you wish. There is no other pace so enchanting and restful as this one. It is achieved only by much practice, checking the pony

An unschooled yearling with the author.

quite hard if it exceeds the speed limit, and letting the reins immediately slack again on achieving it. Any rider who has a constant tight hold on the reins not only will harden the pony's mouth but will never get that beautiful free feeling, the result of a controlled canter, which is the outcome of weeks of gentle stopping and starting by your voice and hands and aids. Again, patience pays dividends.

I never want to see a "green" pony (one that is unschooled) being ridden by a rider standing in the stirrups, or with short stirrups. At this stage you must sit down to your pony, or your buttocks, which do a vast amount in achieving obedience, cannot control the movement of your mount. My idea of riding the unschooled pony on the curb only of its rubber pelham makes it possible from the start to put into the pony's head a fixed idea that it will get hurt if it pulls. Its mouth is tender, and the lightest touch controls it. If it attempts to run away or pull, the curb will stop it. I have never known a pony broken my way to have a bad mouth, and in the past I have sold ponies bought and broken in Argentina that have fetched large sums of money in England, when they had cost me only a few pesos plus the fare to bring them home. These were top-class polo ponies, mouthed exactly as I have described.

6·Preparing for a Ride

BEFORE I TALK ABOUT how to correctly bridle and saddle your pony, I would like to say a word or two about your own equipment and dress. Not everyone can afford very smart and expensive clothes. It is quite essential, however, to have a hard hat or cap in case you are thrown. Nobody, however expert he may be, can be sure he will not unexpectedly be thrown off should the pony get scared. It is always injuries to the head that cause the most trouble.

Jodhpurs seem to be the favorite getup these days for riding, but far too many of them are too tight. If this is the case, the girl has to have a leg-up to get on her pony, or else use a mounting block. This is all wrong. When being fitted in new jodhpurs, try lifting your leg in a bent position. You should be able to lift and bend it comfortably right back on itself up to your chest. If the grip around the knee is too tight, it will hurt you, and if the trousers aren't long enough between the seat and the knee, you will be quite unable to

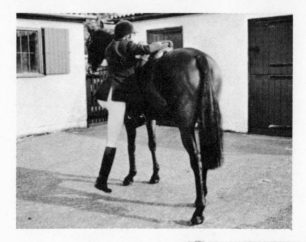

Riding clothes must allow plenty of freedom of movement, especially for mounting.

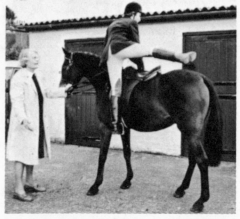

get up onto a big pony easily. With stretch materials, this problem seldom occurs.

If you have a riding jacket, do try to have one that covers your seat. There is nothing so ugly as too short a coat with a large expanse of rear showing.

I used to wear beautifully made divided skirts lined with chamois. They used to be made in brown tweed for ordinary wear and gray flannel for Sundays and go-to-meeting days. Nobody knew they were anything but ordinary skirts, and I could pop onto my pony when I felt like it. They had deep pleats down the front and back and looked very smart.

The jacket should be cut just long enough to hide the seat of the breeches.

Some girls ride in shoes with a small heel; some have jodhpur boots. But whatever you choose, *don't* use rubber-soled soles, or one day you will fall off and your foot will stick in the stirrup iron. This is not likely to happen with ordinary leather-soled shoes.

String or brown leather gloves finish off your equipment for hacking purposes. Myself, I much prefer string gloves. You will need to carry a crop—not to beat the pony with, but to open and shut gates. And if you are schooling a pony to put it on the right leg, it helps to press its shoulder with the crop, as mentioned earlier.

75

Placing the rein over the pony's head ready for bridling.

Opening the pony's mouth with the second and third fingers.

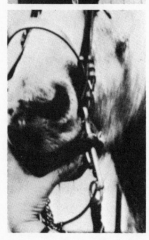

Bit in position for inserting into the pony's mouth.

Now let's talk about bridling and saddling your pony. If it is in the stable, all you have to do to put on its bridle is hold the reins in your right hand and place them over its head; the bridle is held in your left hand. Next, hold the head-piece of the bridle in your right hand and slip it over the front of the pony's face until the noseband is halfway over its nose. Now, holding the bridle steady in this position, take the bit in the palm of your left hand with your forefinger under and thumb over its bar, your hand being open as wide as possible. To make the pony open its mouth easily so that you can insert the bit, put your left forefinger into the pony's mouth behind the lower front teeth. There is a nice empty space there, and you can't get bitten. Press on the lower jaw with your forefinger and the pony's mouth will open. Then, as the bit slips into place, your right hand raises the headpiece of the bridle over the pony's ears. Be careful to push the ears forward gently; if you are rough, you may make the pony nervous about its head for life.

Fasten the throatlatch, just tight enough to prevent the bridle from coming off; do not make it so tight that it half-chokes the pony.

Now, standing with your back to the pony's head, lift the saddle in both hands quite high above the pony's back and lower it gently into position, shifting it about to get it comfortably into place behind the shoulder. Bend down slowly, talking lovingly to the pony, and find the girth from the other side. Fasten the girth loosely at first and make the pony take a step or two. If it hunches its back to buck, keep walking it around until it is accustomed to the cold saddle. In a minute or two, tighten the girth to the required tension.

To mount, stand close to the pony's left shoulder, with your back to its head. Gather the reins up short in your left hand. With your right hand, turn the stirrup iron toward you so that when you are mounted, the smooth flat edge will rest against your leg. Place your foot right up to the arch in the stirrup iron and make a hop or series of hops until you are at right angles to the pony. Press your toe down hard in the iron until it is under the pony's chest where the girth goes. Your left hand now catches on to the tree of the saddle or to a piece of the pony's mane. Your right hand holds the back of the saddle, and with a quick spring you throw your right leg over the saddle and place your foot in the stirrup.

To get your stirrup leathers approximately the right length before mounting, stand by your pony, hold the iron in your left hand, stretch the leather and place the iron under your right armpit. Next stretch your right arm out straight with your hand clenched. Reach to the position where the leather is fixed to the saddle—that is, the bar. Shorten or lengthen the leather until it is this length. When you are mounted, make any adjustment necessary, and change your toe position so that only the ball of your foot is resting on the iron. Twist the iron slightly so that its inside rests across the ball of your foot and against your arch. This prevents the iron from falling off your foot too easily should something unexpected happen.

Take care to get your reins the right length—and by this I mean held lightly in one or two hands to begin with if your pony is fresh, applying very light contact on the pony's mouth. Speak to the pony in an encouraging voice with the command "Walk on," and press your heels on its ribs as you set off. Never start off at a fast pace; wait until the pony has settled down for a few minutes before trying anything fast, or any schooling. Sit up straight, but don't hollow your back. Sit well back in the seat of your saddle, keep your heels well pressed down and your legs will stay in that comfortable position without much effort.

Carry your hand or hands holding the reins about ten inches above the tree of the saddle—not on the pony's withers, as you so often see amateurs doing. Years ago, we were taught "Keep your head well up and your hands and your heels well down." But as I can tell you after years abroad when I spent an average of nine hours a day in the saddle,

Measuring the stirrup-leather length.

there is nothing so uncomfortable and tiring as keeping one's hands well down. The natural position is one you see in cowboy films, in which the reins are held in the right hand about six inches away from your chest and about ten inches above the pommel of the saddle. Your forefinger should be between the two reins, your thumb on the two reins pressed together and your fist closed. Should it be necessary to apply both hands to the reins for extra control, all you have to do is pull the left-hand rein slightly away from your right-hand closed fist, and place your left hand, palm downward, on the left rein, with all four fingers on the rein and your thumb lying along it. It is a one-second job to return it to your right hand, shorten the rein again by pulling it through the slightly opened fist of this hand and once more have both reins held lightly in one hand.

There is only one position of the hands on the reins that makes me see red: the one with the reins held in both hands separately, thumbs on the reins, the four fingers over them and palms turned *upward*. If the pony starts to bolt or buck, with your palms facing upward, you've had it; you would never see such a false position in any country where long hours are spent on horseback. If you like to ride with two hands, your palms should face downward. I had a very large riding school at Oxford years ago. Never once did I allow any of my pupils to use this upward-palm position. And when I trained all the Oxford Indian and English Student Candidates for the Civil Service riding exam, which took place at the Military Academy at Woolwich, every year it was my pupils who got the best marks in their examination. So even military examiners must approve of my methods.

The secret of happy and comfortable riding is to be ready for anything at all times, and to know also that your pony is with you in mind and body all the time. Relax and enjoy the time spent on its back and you and your pony will be better company for each other.

7·More Advanced Training

HAVING GOTTEN YOUR PONY to do the simple walk, trot and canter, relying on the aids and voice more than on the bit, you must eventually let it gallop. This should not be done until you have completed about six weeks of training at the slow gaits. Most ponies don't get enough practice at the slow speeds before their young riders allow them to go all out. This excites the pony, and unless it is brought back to its slow canter every time it has a short burst of faster work, it will forget its manners one day and not be so easy to check, especially when ridden in the company of other ponies.

I believe that this controlled canter should be practiced for weeks among other ponies. Let your friends gallop past you, but you keep your pony at its slow pace. You will never regret spending a lot of time on this exercise. In Argentina the ponies are kept at this for three months. They are given to an outpost man for this period, even though they may have been broken by another native. Even the ponies I

broke for the company were, by order, made to do the slow work of the outpost man—which is, of course, just riding around the herds, twisting and turning among them, opening and shutting gates; carrying injured lambs back to the *estancia* and often also the job of riding into town for supplies.

The idea was to give the maximum amount of slow work. This so conditioned the pony to these slow speeds that it naturally set off at that pace and kept it up very often for hours at a time without much effort or control on the part of the rider.

This slow work is also the best possible thing for getting a pony fit. It gets rid of its tummy if it is out at grass, sweats the dirt gently out of its coat and is the best way to ensure that when it *is* allowed to gallop, its wind is ready to take it.

Now let's assume the pony has been ridden everywhere slowly for at least one month. It has been made to back routinely every time you stop, and is absolutely quiet to mount and dismount. If it isn't you have not carried out instructions.

Standing still while being mounted is taught by tying the pony to a tree while you mount. If it tries to walk off, it is checked by its halter rope, which is attached to the tree.

The next stage is to hold the rope in your hand after it has been passed around a branch; then as soon as you are settled in the saddle you can drop it, and pick it up again by leaning forward and getting hold of the halter end.

When you mount, always exaggerate the time you take before you wish to move off. Tighten your girth; adjust your leathers. Wave your arms around a bit, and generally get the pony used to standing still quite a long time. A pony that is allowed to set off almost as soon as you have one foot in the stirrup is a menace and a danger to your safety, for one day you will get dragged.

And since I am on the subject of being dragged, do remember never to put in an upright position the little hinge that holds the stirrup leather to the bar of the saddle. If you do and fall off, the leather may not be released. Should your leathers fall off while you are riding as a result of your having left the little hinge down, it will teach you to keep your legs in the right position next time, for if the leather does come off it means your legs are much too far back on the saddle flap.

When you first let a pony gallop, don't wave your legs and kick hard with your heels in an effort to increase its speed. Make the increase very slowly, simply by urging the pony on with your voice and by moving your buttocks firmly backward and forward in the seat of the saddle. The pony will feel this movement and automatically increase its speed.

Your reins for this speed should be in two hands, as I have already described. To begin with, you must never lean forward over the pony's neck, or stand in your stirrups, or one day the pony will put its head between its legs and buck, and off you will go. All you need to do is lean slightly forward, sitting in the center of the saddle more than in the seat. When you wish to stop, say "Shhh" and return to the seat of the saddle and lean very slightly back, putting pressure on the reins. Only if the pony is out of control do you need to stand up in your stirrups, lowering your hands onto its shoulders and pulling hard on the bit. If the pony has been mouthed my way, you will never find yourself in this ghastly situation. The word "Shhh" will be ingrained in its mind, and it will slide its back legs up to its front legs in order to stop and get some sugar—for I always give sugar when training a pony to stop quickly from a gallop.

Always make a great fuss over your pony at all times. Ponies love being rubbed underneath the mane as well as being stroked and patted and addressed lovingly. If only more people would talk to their horses, what a difference it would make! I see too many heels and far too many crops being used for my liking.

The next step in training, a very important one, is to teach your pony to "passage," or sidestep, freely; this is very useful for sidling up to gates. It is very easy to teach if you have neck-reined your pony, as all you do is keep neck-reining it the way you want to go, and use your heels or a twig to push the pony or tap it lightly over the opposite ribs or quarters, at the same time urging it slightly on so that it doesn't passage with one front leg going behind the other. They should pass in front of each other. I always use the word "Over" in a high-pitched tone, as that is the word you have probably been using when you're cleaning out your stable and want the pony to get over out of the way while you are working.

It should do the half-passage first, which is going half-forward and sidewise. When your pony is good at that, move to the full passage, which is going straight sidewise, not forward at all. If you have difficulty in getting your mount to do this exercise, get a friend to push the pony as you give the commands and aids. Give it sugar when it does it right.

Now the pony must learn to break into a canter from a standstill. It puts me into a rage to watch a pony that needs terrific waving of elbows and frantic kicking with the heels to make it break into a canter. The rider must have pep in her own character to achieve this break easily, A dull, phlegmatic child will seldom get anywhere with this exercise.

You must apply both heels hard simultaneously to the pony's ribs, your reins must be slack and your seat must work with your thighs, urging the pony into a canter by pressure. If it trots, check it and start again. If you have the slow, lazy, fat type of pony, you may need a little twig or your crop to help you. But I hate all forms of painful punishment, and I hope my readers will have enough character to achieve this movement without resorting to the whip.

Always use the same word, in a high-pitched tone, which will wake a pony out of its dreams. Before attempting to break into a canter, you must collect the pony's head up into the cantering position, especially if you have had long, hanging reins and have been indulging in a dreamy walk. It is the gathering up of the reins that excites the pony. Then as soon as you loosen the reins, the pony should spring off. If ever you need your pony for gymkhanas or polo, you will know you haven't a chance of doing well without this instant break into a canter or gallop.

Walking can be done at many speeds. There is nothing so tiring as a slow walk, especially when you're coming home after a long day in the saddle. You must teach your pony the extended walk, which is urging it on faster and faster until it is just behind the trotting speed. Should it break into a trot, check it quickly and then urge it on to the full extended walk. *Never* allow your pony to half-trot, half-walk in a jig-jog; it is killing for your back. Either make it do a slow trot so you can sit down to it in the saddle, as South Americans do, or keep it to a fast walk. If the pony jigs, correct it lightly with the reins in one hand, say "Steady" soothingly to it and run the finger and thumb of your other hand down either side of the mane. This will often stop jig-jogging more quickly than anything else.

Now teach your pony to have a polo mallet or some such object waved all around it. Nothing steadies a pony more quickly than this. Turn the pony in circles in the direction of the stick and pretend to hit a ball. This training will help enormously in gymkhanas when you have barrel races, egg races, and so on.

Put up a few posts and teach the pony to bend, being sure it changes legs as it changes directions. If it doesn't do this, you haven't done enough cantering in small circles to make it handy. Go back to that and practice some hours at it. Next accustom your pony to cantering and, later, galloping with you bending right forward over its neck, the reins lightly controlling its mouth, bending the pony by shifting the weight of your body, and pressing it with your legs and thighs. To get a pony supple and handy, you must work hard at twisting, turning, stopping and so on. This is not something that can be taught in a day.

Dismounting the way I am going to tell you about is much safer, I think, for children than only taking one foot out of the stirrup and dismounting army fashion, which is to leave the nearside foot in the stirrup until you are down. I always taught my pupils to dismount by placing both arms outstretched on either side of the pony's neck and doing a swing-off with both legs stretched out straight, as one vaults over the horse at school in the gym. Get your legs up high and let your heels click as they meet when you first start; then even if the pony is moving you can do this safely. It is most useful for quick work at gymkhanas. The whole secret is to get your arms and head well down beside the pony's neck as you come off. But to get the swing you must lean back first, then forward and get your legs up almost in one movement. Speed is essential. Both feet must be out of the stirrups, of course, before you start. Incidentally, this is one thing you don't see in Argentina. The Argentines dismount army fashion, with the near left foot remaining in the stirrup iron.

Jumping interests many children, but in this book I am going to ignore the modern methods of shortening your stirrups and perching up on your horse's withers from beginning to end. I think that is a very unsafe method of teaching a child or a pony to jump. Many people will criticize me, but I and my many hundreds of pupils have learned my way, and were happy.

The danger of leaning forward is that on landing, your pony may not like the weight or feel of your hands on its withers and put its head between its legs , and off you will go. Or if it doesn't do that, it may "peck" or stumble, and you will also land on your nose in the forward position. I suggest teaching a pony to jump by putting up very low poles and leading it over them, jumping them yourself. If you jumped them and the pony didn't, get a friend to tap its backside with a twig or wave her arms. One or two taps on its quarters will soon teach it to jump. Next, you ride and let your friend hold the pony and jump while leading it. Lastly, do it alone. You must have big wings on the jump to teach a pony, because if you let the pony get away with running out and not jumping, you have made a big error in training. Animals must never be allowed to get away with things you don't want them to do. Patience, kindness and occasionally great firmness are unbreakable rules for training anything with four legs.

When you first start to jump, use the neckband of a martingale to hang on to, to stop yourself from jerking the pony's mouth. The hold on its mouth should be the lightest possible, and it must never be jerked. At first its jumping will be uncollected, but a "green" pony is best left to jump that way. You would be surprised how often horse and rider come to grief because the rider thought she knew more than the pony. If the pony is left to collect itself when it gets on the wrong leg or when its stride is wrong, all will be well and in most cases the wrong will be righted.

I love to see the free way riders from Italy and Spain allow their mounts to have their heads and their freedom when negotiating difficult obstacles. It makes me squirm to see some riders force their horses to go so slowly that they simply haven't the speed to clear the obstacle. I know a headstrong animal must be forcibly controlled. But I would like to see more horses and ponies schooled to do the natural slow canter at all times, with encouragement to go faster only when the jump is being approached. Some of today's show jumpers are a sorry sight with their tight martingales, dropped nosebands and lack of suppleness, which prevents them from turning quickly on difficult corners. Most of them could do with a little polo training before being returned to the jumping ring.

Far too much hanging on to the bit is seen; but that is driving your horse into its bit, which I have disagreed with from the beginning. I want a horse or pony *behind* its bit, so it can be urged into it at fast speeds. In this way you have something in reserve, and you have not tired out your mount.

To learn to jump, you must know something about the number of paces required to take the horse over easily. I always figure it is "One, two and a half," and jump. The rider should in the early stages lean forward going up to the jump, and as the pony is in the air lean back. Thus, if the pony stumbles you have a good chance of staying put, or at least not being thrown hard. It is also easier on the pony's front legs, and you are far less likely to jab its mouth on landing. As you gain experience and confidence, and provided your pony is well schooled, you can do the forward seat as is done in the show ring today. Until you are quite sure of the number of paces and where the pony should take off, don't attempt to teach it to jump. Learn on an experienced one first.

I well remember a cow pony in Argentina that had never seen a jump before which, when I put up jumps, cleared 5.6 feet the first time and then rose to 6.3 feet without apparent effort. It was like flying. I had visions of bringing it home and winning everything in the jumping ring. But a friend of the manager's came to see the *estancia* and saw me jump it. He begged to have a try. I was dead set against it, but was ordered to give up the pony. The man got on, and in a blustering manner went for the highest jump. The pony lost its head, jumped wildly and knocked it down. It never jumped again, and even trembled in terror if it so much as saw a jump.

A young rider and her pony going over crossbars.

So now you can see how careful you have to be not to unnerve the pony by jabbing its mouth—or for that matter, falling off under its nose and jabbing its mouth by holding on to the reins as you fall. I know it is said you should never let go of the reins, but you can hurt the pony too much sometimes by being dragged on its mouth, especially if it's a pony that has been mouthed my way with a curb.

When you are out riding, jump every little ditch and obstacle you come to; it is all good practice.

When you are jumping, put an extra rein on the pelham

and ride the pony on the upper ring, not the curb. The mouth is far too sensitive to take the risk of bad hands and jerks from an inexperienced rider. Far too many riders balance on their horses' mouths. I used to take all reins away from my pupils when they were beginners at jumping. They held the neckband at first and then folded their arms. It gave them grip and balance, and that is what I want my readers to develop. Naturally, I did not use inexperienced horses or ponies for this work, and would never advise anyone to try it with a young pony. You must give the pony confidence to jump at the right time, and you must have no fear yourself. Fear is extremely catching. Therefore, only good riders should break in and school ponies.

Once the pony has gotten accustomed to low jumps, try to find something with a ditch in front of it. There is nothing as good for a pony as learning to spread itself. A ditch in front of the jump is far better to start with than one after the jump. If you can't find a ditch, put a pole in front of the jump, about one foot high and painted white. But never train with fixed jumps or you and the pony will risk broken necks. Only experienced ponies should attempt stiles or fixed jumps.

Practice brings perfection; it never pays to hurry when teaching a pony to jump. And for goodness' sake, don't do it so much that your pony gets sick of it. A stale pony refuses jumps and then probably has to be punished, and the whole rapport between pony and owner is lost.

A *foal* receives the breathing greeting as its mother and the author look on.

8·Faults and Vices

I THINK I HAVE SAID ENOUGH about young ponies and the gentle training that leads them step by step to becoming smooth rides and reliable mounts at all times. If a pony is excitable or bad-tempered after it is trained my way, I lay the blame fairly and squarely at the doorstep of its young owner, for she has been too impatient; she has not made the pony stay at its slow work long enough. If the pony is bad-tempered, its owner has either been rough in her commands, or brushed it too roughly, or not been firm enough with it when it has tried to kick or bite as a youngster. Nearly all foals need to be handled firmly.

My little half-Arab foal kicked me a few minutes after she was born, and I thought at first it was by mistake, but when she came galloping past me like a jet plane and I received a hard kick on my knee, I realized that if this was the foal's idea of play, it was not mine; so the next time I went into the field, I was waiting for this lightning attack. I had a rope with me, and as she passed me I not only stepped aside as she kicked out, but gave her a hard whack on her quarters with the end of the rope. She stopped and turned around, and a look of complete surprise registered on her face. She came up to me and sniffed me. Then I sniffed back through my nostrils with my hands behind my back, and we called it quits. From that day on she has never done it again.

Had I not been actually hit by her hooves, I might have just thought it was play and left it at that, and she might have gotten more domineering than ever, and become nasty-tempered. All animals have to respect their owners, and this tiny mite had come into this world with a superiority complex, and had decided to rule human beings. She soon learned better.

If ponies are taught respect from an early age, and given sugar as soon as they can eat it, they soon become so tame that breaking them is no trouble at all. But never let them run after you when you have given them a tidbit, and threaten you with ears laid back because you haven't any more. I always make my foals and adult ponies come to me. I whistle to them, and when they come they get fed.

Usually the old mother teaches the foal, and the foal soon recognizes the association of whistle and sugar and comes easily. This keeps ponies from being difficult to catch in the field. So many young owners have to gather together a number of friends or their parents to help them catch their pony. What a curse this must be! They nearly all tell me the same story. The pony comes for food, and then as their hand goes out to catch hold of the halter, the pony darts away.

Well, this is simple to cure. Attach quite a long, light chain dragging on the pony, and put your foot on it. Feed the pony, and then when it tries to dart away, it can't because you have it firmly held by your foot. It hasn't seen you bend down, so has no idea why it can't get away. After a few tries like this, the idea of escape vanishes. I prefer an ordinary large collar for this rather than a halter, because a halter is inclined to rub the nose, and a collar doesn't. Have

The author in the process of teaching her half-Arab foal to stop kicking.

it tight enough to prevent the pony from getting it over its head. If the pony turns its heels on you when you try to catch it, you can pick up the loose chain and yank the animal around. Again, surprise at not being able to kick will make the pony realize you are in charge.

Always pet it and feed it with tidbits when it does come head first, not heels first, to you. In Argentina the horses are all put into a corral, and on the word *"Forme"* they all line up to face their masters. If a young one fails to do so, the old horses nip its quarters until it does; it soon learns what to do.

You may think it is dangerous to have the pony drag a chain until it learns to let you catch it, but I have used this method on many ponies and never had any damage done. They soon learn to avoid treading on the chain. The only danger comes from other horses' treading on it, but this is remote; horses seldom tread on chains. Be sure to have it long enough to prevent you from getting within range of the pony's heels when you are bending to pick it up. A chain lasts longer than a rope.

The following is an example of a more difficult problem. A child should never attempt to tame such a dangerous pony.

Star was a half-Arab yearling no one could catch. He would jump everything and if cornered in a barn would rear and behave so dangerously that the idea of catching him was given up. He was to be destroyed.

I was challenged to catch him in front of television cameras and accepted.

He was driven with another pony into a barn, and the other pony was quickly driven out. The terror in Star's eyes showed this attack on his freedom had been tried many times. I spoke to him continuously in a low, soft voice, and gently maneuvered him into a corner. He always went to the right, which meant I was attempting to get near him on his off side, not the usual near side, and he always turned his heels to me.

I knew the risk I was taking, always being within reach of his heels, and I couldn't use the breathing trick. He felt his heels were the best defense against me or any human being.

Time and again I managed to get my left hand on his quarters to stroke them; in every case he panicked and reared his way out of the corner, plunging wildly around the barn. Food did not interest him. After two hours I placed a rolled-up piece of string in my left palm, because by this time I had been able to stroke him up to his withers, talking gently all the time. I dropped one end of the string down his nearside shoulder and with my right hand picked up the end. The string was about six feet long. I quickly tied a knot —unfortunately, only a slipknot—before he reared himself to freedom once more. This time there was the danger of the dragging string's catching on something and closing the noose on his neck. To my relief, I got him into the corner again and completed a safe knot; but how to change the string to a safe rope was my next task. I attached a rope to the end of the string and held it around a post. At the first

Two students waiting for a word from the author.

feel of restriction, Star reared repeatedly—nearly fell over backward—and the worst happened—the post gave way.

Once again I got Star into the corner he had chosen as his refuge. This time I got my left hand under his mane and started the gentle tickling all ponies are soothed by; his eyes temporarily closed. I managed to get the string around

The author with slipknot around Star's neck.

his nose and joined to the loop around his neck, making a temporary halter. I turned his face to mine and breathed up his nose. The result was amazing: all fear left him, and he followed me. I put a halter on him, and Star was finally caught after three hours of gentle battle.

The next day, again on television, I gave him his first breaking-in. He learned to walk, trot and back-step on command on a loose rope. I put a light felt saddle on him; I had him lift his legs, which he quickly did on command and reward, and Star was tamed.

I found him a home with a little girl of 2½ who sits happily on his back. Lots of children hug him, he has won many prizes in hand in shows and when old enough he will be the mount of the little girl. They will grow up together. All fear has left him.

On this subject of vices, watch your pony for "wind sucking." I once turned out a valuable pony in a field with an old cart horse which I didn't know had this vice, and in no time at all my pony had picked it up too. A horse is windsucking when it gets hold of a gate or fence with its front teeth and bites and sucks in air at the same time. One remedy is to put a very tight collar around the animal's neck. Another is to make the posts unpalatable by painting them with creosote. This is an excellent deterrent! But with a bad case you may have to keep the pony in and muzzle it, taking off the muzzle only for feeding and watering.

Hard mouths can be made manageable again by reschooling, but this is best left to an expert, as few young owners have sufficient expertise for it.

When the pony gets used to being lightly and comfortably controlled, you will find that its bad mouth was really bad head and neck carriage, and when this is corrected you will have no further trouble.

It seems to me that an excessive number of people these days are using the iniquitous dropped noseband to keep the pony from opening its mouth to show discomfort or getting its tongue over the bit—both of which show bad initial mouthings. A pony that has been properly mouthed when broken has no need to open its mouth, resisting the action of the bit. If this happens, it means the pony's head is in the wrong position, either held too low for control or too high for the bit to put the correct pressure on the bars of the mouth, which would bend the pony's head to the right position.

Unable to open their mouths, ponies then rear to get rid of the pain of the bit, coupled very often with the pressure

Star now totally unafraid.

of the rider's knees on the saddle, usually with too-short stirrup leathers. The pressure to go forward should come from the rider's calves and seat rather than knees—not forgetting the use of voice, so vital in the training or riding of any pony.

The word "contact" produces shivers in me; it means a constant hold on the pony's mouth with hands and arms so stiff that the mouth quickly hardens and the sensitivity of the pony to the slightest touch on the bit quickly lessens.

The answer, in my opinion, is to remouth a rearing pony and get its neck bending correctly. I have found that a rider can achieve this by using a Gloster noseband as a bitless bridle (keeping a bit in the mouth only for an emergency), then placing the extra neck strap in the position that achieves the correct and comfortable head position.

Using the Gloster noseband as a bitless bridle.

The neck strap in place, complementing the Gloster noseband, to achieve the correct head position.

The Gloster noseband used with a standing martingale.

The noseband can be given extra power if the reins from the rider's hands are run through the two small rings under the chin and attached by a ring to a standing martingale about two feet long. This acts as a draw rein, and the extra neck strap can be adjusted to suit the pony. This, however, should be used only in an extreme case. Normally the neck strap and the spring in the noseband very quickly produce the required control.

Should the neck strap slip too far down the neck, tighten it until it stays in the required position. Ponies that were going to be destroyed for rearing or backing have been saved by this invention, and bad hands on the part of the rider have been alleviated by the resulting ease of control —which makes light hands a necessity. I firmly believe if all ponies were taught to neck-rein instead of being pulled around on their mouths, rearing could be stopped in the breaking-in and schooling days.

Very often, if the pony hasn't too bad a mouth, the simple change from a snaffle to riding on one rein on the curb is quite sufficient; but you must leave the pony for at least an hour a day remouthing itself in the stable.

You must give daily schooling in turning and bending; and most important of all, don't let the pony gallop for six weeks. Bad temperament can quickly be cured by a placid, gentle rider who keeps her seat in the saddle with her legs controlling the pony and firmly but persistently making the pony perform at a slow canter in small circles and on the straight. There is no shortcut. Bitting and daily schooling are the only ways.

In the same way, when a pony suddenly whips around and tries to make off for home, which is a very common vice, the only way to handle it is to turn it around and around in small circles very gently but firmly until it gets slightly giddy and loses its sense of direction; then let it go on the way you want and you seldom have any more trouble.

Vice is not a thing I advise a young rider to tackle. With the roads as dangerous as they are today, it just isn't worth risking. But there always comes a time in every rider's experience when the ideas of your mount don't coincide with your own, and if at that time you win, you seldom have any more trouble. But if you let the pony take you home against your will even once, it may require an almighty battle of wills to keep it from doing so the next time too.

Shying is one of these bad habits, and to cure shying you have to drive the pony right up to whatever it is shying at, and if possible make the pony tread on it. I mean this in regard to a piece of paper or some such fluttering object, things which almost always cause shying in a nervous pony. Tightening your reins and gripping the pony with your thighs, in my opinion, make matters worse; it gives the pony the impression that you are nervous too. Sit firmly down by all means, but try to keep only a light hold on the pony, being at the same time ready to hold it harder should it shy.

I have given confidence to many a shying pony by letting it approach what I knew would make it shy on quite a slack rein, and with my body relaxed as well. The shying has decreased steadily.

To be able to do this you must ride by balance, as a leap to the right or left would otherwise send you off the pony. If your balance is not good, you will have to grip to stay on. Good balance is learned only from twisting and turning a pony at speed, and by having a very supple body yourself. I used to get my pupils supple by teaching them to lean right back the first time they were learning to canter. That made their seats stay in the saddle rather than do that awful "bump, up, bump" that you nearly always see a beginner doing. It made the small of the back loosen so that their seats stayed in the saddle, and from the waist up they went with the motion of the horse.

By this method you can teach people to canter in very few lessons; once you learn this way to go loosely relaxed with

An American Quarter Horse standing quietly while its master picks up the mail.

your pony's action, you can soon do the same thing sitting up straight. Try this out, you beginners. You have to lean quite a long way back, holding on to the tree of the saddle to steady yourself and give you confidence.

Beginners lose their nerve very quickly after a bad tumble. I remember once in Argentina a neighbor called with a new pony he had been breaking in and asked me to ride it and see how I liked it—a thing I never willingly do; I always prefer to break horses for myself. However, I did get on it so as not to offend him and took it out in the camp for a ride. His bull terrier accompanied the horse. When we got a little way out, the dog started chasing the sheep. I put the horse into a gallop and leaned forward in an effort to make it go faster to catch this wretched dog. The pony, badly broken in, put its head between its legs and bucked as if it were in a rodeo. Off I went, clean over its head onto my own! I held on to the reins and was dragged for more than half a mile. For the first time in my life, I lost my nerve for a few days. Let this be a warning to those who stand in their stirrups on a young horse not properly trained. After that I stuck to my own unbroken horses; they were nicer to ride!

Traffic-shy ponies are very unsafe. The cure is to lead the pony through dense traffic with another which doesn't mind, always keeping the shy one on the inside. The very best thing to do is find a small paddock near a busy road and arrange to turn the pony out there for a week. Soon it won't even look at traffic.

TRAILERING

So many ponies make a fuss at being asked to go into a trailer that I feel wrong methods may have been used to try to achieve this.

First of all, bandage all legs, padding them with cotton batting, and put on knee caps for safety's sake.

Put a very strong halter on the pony and attach it to a very long lungeing rein or strong rope.

Place the trailer close to a wall if one is available; otherwise fit sides to the ramp.

If possible, put the trailer on a fairly steep slope, to make the ramp much flatter for the pony.

Attach the long rope or lungeing rein to the halter under the jaw; then pass it through the ring at the driver's end of the box, walk to the side of the pony and with possibly two people on the rope, gently apply a firm pull. There should be plenty of straw on the ramp. Don't attempt to drive or help the pony in any way to mount the ramp; just keep the pull on the halter steady and wait. Usually in about five minutes the pony will give a big leap onto the ramp. Then quickly gather up the slack in the rope to maintain the tension on the halter until the pony is inside. Then tie it up and give it a reward of food—a carrot or sugar.

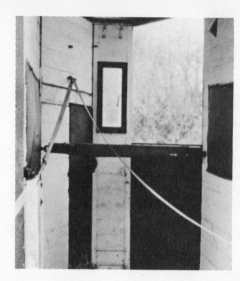

The lungeing rein is attached to the pony's halter and then passed through a ring at the driver's end of the trailer.

Keep the pull on the halter steady, and soon the pony will jump onto the ramp.

When the pony steps onto the ramp, keep pulling steadily but gently on the lungeing rein until the animal is in the trailer.

If the pony seems to need help, some people lift one front foot onto the ramp; but this could be dangerous, since the pony might leap forward and knock the person over, so I don't advise it.

Leave the pony in the trailer for about two hours. Then back or walk it out and repeat the process. The pony learns quickly to board without fuss.

Author gently caressing under the pony's mane. Note mouth of pony moving in contentment.

A foal by its mother's side.

9·Breeding

No BOOK ON PONIES would be complete without a short chapter on breeding for a foal. Before they outgrow their ponies, many children, if they own a mare, have bred her and have a foal which is growing with them. By the time their small pony has been outgrown they have a bigger one growing up.

The experience gained in riding the small pony is now going to be used to advantage when the new foal is between two and three years old and ready to do light work.

The pony mare is usually sent for about two months to the stud, unless there is a light Arab or another suitable pony traveling the district, which makes it possible to serve the pony at your own home. The mare carries the foal for eleven months, roughly 340 days, although great variations have been known.

It is amazing how a "maiden," a mare that has never had a foal before, can look as slim and fit as if she were not going to have one. I well remember how one of my Argentine

Clover Honey and her foal.

ponies came to England and played fast polo; then in between chukkers she lay down and delivered a foal. We had no idea at all she was pregnant, and apparently the fast work with its twisting and turning did *her* no harm at all, but she produced an awful sort of cart-horse foal. Normally I wouldn't work a pony at all in the eleventh month, and only very lightly the month before. When she begins to show she is pregnant by her increase in size, she should not be ridden fast or jumped. But steady exercise does her good. A mare that has been pampered seldom foals as easily as one that has been worked in, say, chains on the farm, or ridden gently. It preserves her muscle tone, and keeps her digestion healthy. She should be fed well in winter to nourish the foal to come, but not overfed.

If she is in at night during winter, alfalfa hay is the best feed, because it is rich in vitamins and minerals, which makes for good bone growth in the baby to come. If she is to foal indoors, she should sleep in the foaling stall some weeks ahead of time. I personally prefer to have my foals born in May, when the natural grass is available and when the nights are warm. Seldom does a foal born at this time of year need bringing in at all. It gets accustomed to the variations of weather, and can, unless there is some exceptionally bad weather, stay out all next winter.

Try to handle the flanks and mammary glands as much as possible to accustom the mare to this, so that when the little foal is born the mother will not be too ticklish to allow it to suck. When the time is approaching for the foal to be born, the mare's mammary glands swell and may exhibit "waxing." The gland extends beyond its normal shape, and fluid begins to drip from the teat of the gland. A clear sort of wax can be pressed from the teat, but I never do this. The mare keeps away from other stock, and becomes uneasy. My little mare Florin felt so lonely when she was having her first foal that she came up to me in the field, lay down and had her baby right at my feet. My son Patrick got out his camera and

Bold Ruler, a famous Thoroughbred racehorse.

took a photo of it two minutes after it was born. I was so surprised! In no time at all both the mother and foal were standing up. A very short time afterward the mother passed the "afterbirth," which is the membrane in which the baby foal lives before it is born.

After the foal is born, its umbilical cord will break naturally from the placenta. The cord must then be dipped in iodine solution to prevent "navel ill," a disease that can enter through the cord. It is best to let the cord break naturally because as long as it is intact, the foal is getting blood from the placenta.

Should the mare appear to be straining very hard before the foal is born and no progress is being made, it is best to call your veterinarian. Most ponies foal alone, but some need professional assistance. Be sure, immediately after the foal is born, that it can breathe freely. Wipe any mucus or bits of membrane away from its mouth and nose. If the mare pays no attention to the foal, as she may not do if it is her first, carry it around to her head, and she will begin to lick it dry. Should she not do so it must be dried with towels, but very few mares neglect their offspring.

Some mares don't seem to have any milk, or very little, and I had to rear one of my foals on cow's milk with sugar added to it. Normally the foal will suck its mother very soon after birth, but occasionally the mare bites the foal. Then the owner would have to either tie the mare up or hold her by her head four or five times a day while the foal nurses. I think mares bite at first because their mammary glands are tender, for later they don't make any fuss.

When the foal is about three months old the mare can begin light work again. Shut the foal up or keep it in a paddock with another one while its mother is away or it might try to jump out.

Don't allow the mother to return to her foal and suckle it if she is hot; get her well cooled down and rested first.

When the foal is six months old it can be weaned from its

mother, as it will be eating well by then. If the mother is going to breed every year, she will be returned to the stud three days after foaling and the foal will accompany her. She will come into heat every three to four weeks.

You may breed an ordinary horse or pony to foal at any time of year; but if you are breeding Thoroughbreds, try to get them to foal as soon after the first of the year as possible. A Thoroughbred's age is counted from January 1; so a Thoroughbred foal born on December 31 would still be one year old the next day.

Handle a foal from an early age and get it accustomed to people; then it will never be shy or mean.

The author welcomes a foal into the world.

An Appaloosa stallion.

10·Manners Make the Rider

I FEEL VERY STRONGLY about riders and their manners. Since I am a motorist as well as a rider, I often feel a bit annoyed when I slow down to a stop or crawling pace to let a horse or pony pass and the rider doesn't even bother to give me a smile. Try to remember that a little courtesy goes a long way.

Near my home we have a common. It is a big common, and recently the villagers went to great trouble and expense to flatten out the surface, so that people could enjoy themselves on it. But do the riders of the district respect this piece of open space? No! Some gallop full out on the natural green footpaths, leaving great hoofmarks that fill with water, creating mud everywhere, so that the pedestrians have to walk on the longer grass. This shows lack of consideration for everyone, and only people with bad manners would behave in this way. If there is a pretty spot in your town, preserve it for everyone; don't spoil it selfishly.

Recently I caught a child jumping the benches on the common, and her pony was a bad jumper. One by one she broke the backs of the seats, and had demolished two before I stopped her. Only bad-mannered riders do this—riders who ought to know better. Never join their ranks. Everyone loves to see ponies and their riders. If they ride with consideration for others, they are welcome in most places.

As much as possible, ride on grass borders, not on footpaths. And never ride at night; it is dangerous.

Ride your horse so as to face *oncoming* traffic, and if you ever lead another one, have it safely on your *inside*. I am always terrified by the risks some riding schools take when the instructress leads a small child on a pony on her outside. That pony has only to swerve for the child to be under a car. At other times I see an instructress riding at the head of the string of ponies instead of behind or at least in the middle. How could she possibly avoid a mishap if she wasn't even watching her pupils?

When there is traffic, experienced riders should ride in single file. You never know when your pony might shy into a car. If the driver of a car has any sense or decency, he will always give horses a wide berth; but he may not possess these attributes.

In a hunt, one often sees a lot of bad manners. People in too great a hurry galloping wildly through gates, not only frightening shy horses and nervous riders, but often covering others with mud. There is no fox in the world that goes so fast that the followers cannot slow down through gates. And if you are last, you simply *must* shut the gate. Remember always, you have no *right* to go over the farmers' land; it is only their courtesy that makes it possible. In the same way, footpaths with stiles are not for riders. I have often had young riders knock down my stiles and plow up my footpaths, and when brought to task declare they thought they were riding on a right-of-way. Learn the difference between a bridle path and a footpath.

Never gallop among stock; you may cause sheep and cattle to lose their young. Always keep to the outside edge of cornfields and hayfields, and don't jump through and break down farmers' hedges. If you want to practice jumps, you can always put up a pole at home or jump a fallen tree in the woods.

If your pony kicks, keep right out of everyone's way, and tie a piece of red ribbon on its tail so that others will know the risk they are taking if they come too close. Your pony can kick another pony and wreck the other girl's enjoyment by making it lame, or you can break someone's leg.

If you are at a gymkhana, be sporting. The girl who barges into someone in Musical Chairs may win the race by foul means, but will not be liked. Train your pony so beautifully that its suppleness and your skill in handling it are the factors that give you a ribbon. If you lose, don't go around saying everyone cheated. Try again next time, having spent the time in between the events teaching your pony and yourself to be better. Very often the old, clever pony can beat the much more expensive pony by being steady and well behaved.

Don't come home after being with horses all day and sit in your mother's living room without first taking off your horsy clothes; you may still carry the scent of the stable on your clothes and boots. Remember ponies are delightful creatures in every way, but we don't invite them onto our living-room chairs! And be sure to bathe well after your day's sport.

Above all, don't talk horses, horses, horses all day. Much as people love them, they are not a topic of interesting conversation from 9 A.M. to 9 P.M. every day.

If you remember all these do's and don'ts, you and your pony will be liked everywhere you go.

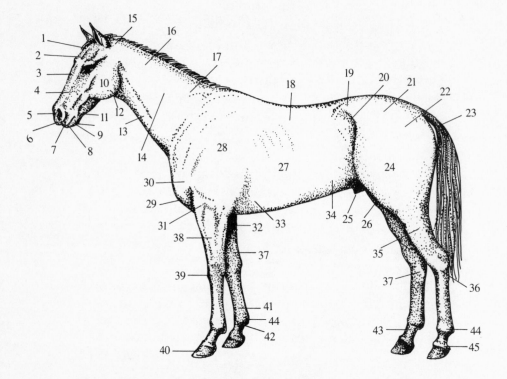

GENERAL CONFORMATION AND POINTS OF THE HORSE.
(1) Forelock. (2) Forehead. (3) Face. (4) Bridge of nose. (5) Nostril. (6) Muzzle. (7) Upper lip. (8) Lower lip. (9) Under lip. (10) Cheek, jaw, or jowl. (11) Chin groove. (12) Throatlatch. (13) Jugular groove. (14) Neck. (15) Poll. (16) Crest. (17) Withers. (18) Back. (19) Loin. (20) Point of hip. (21) Croup. (22) Buttock. (23) Dock. (24) Thigh. (25) Flank. (26) Stifle. (27) Barrel. (28) Shoulder. (29) Point of shoulder. (30) Chest. (31) Arm. (32) Elbow. (33) Girth. (34) Abdomen. (35) Gaskin. (36) Hock. (37) Chestnut. (38) Forearm. (39) Knee. (40) Hoof. (41) Cannon. (42) Ergot. (43) Pastern. (44) Fetlock. (45) Coronet.

·Glossary

BALDING GIRTH   a girth designed to prevent slippage on a horse with a badly shaped belly. It is divided into three equal pieces and twisted in two places. When in use, the pieces lie flat on the horse's belly, and the twists help keep the girth in place.

BIT   used to communicate with the horse and to help encourage correct head carriage and all-around balance. It is the steel or rubber part of the bridle which is put into the horse's mouth. The bit lies on the bars of the mouth (the space between the incisors and molars). In general, a thicker bit is gentler because its pressure is distributed over a wider area.

BOWED TENDON   a swelling or bulge behind the cannon bone caused by severe strain on (and/or tearing of) the flexor tendon in the cannon area of the horse's leg (between the knee and fetlock or the hock and fetlock). The tendon sheath has torn away from the tendon, and there is bleeding inside it. This condition is seen primarily on forelegs but occasionally on a hind leg. If a bowed tendon is suspected, a veterinarian should be consulted.

BOX STALL   a roomy enclosure in a barn where a horse can be kept at night or when not in use. It can be a minimum of ten feet square but is usually twelve feet square. Foaling stalls should be larger (fourteen to sixteen feet square).

BRIDLE   the piece of tack designed to hold the bit in a horse's mouth. It is made up of several parts: the headpiece, throatlatch, browband, cheekpieces, and noseband.

CANTER   a three-beat gait which is faster than the trot and slower than the gallop. If a horse is circling left it should be in a left lead, in which the order of limbs striking the ground is as follows: 1. right hind leg; 2. left hind leg and right foreleg simultaneously; 3. left foreleg. The three beats are followed by a moment of suspension when all four legs are off the ground before the sequence begins again. In a right lead, the left hind leg would begin the sequence.

CONFORMATION   the physical makeup or structure of a horse.

COOLER   a fishnet blanket designed to absorb moisture and allow the passage of air to the coat so that a horse will dry faster after heavy exercise.

CURB BIT   a bit that is more severe than a snaffle. The mouthpiece has an inverted U-shaped rise in the middle which takes some pressure off the horse's tongue and applies it to the roof of the mouth. The mouthpiece is joined to shanks of varying length with loops at the ends to which the reins are attached. The longer the shanks, the more severe the bit. A curb bit can apply pressure to several places: the bars of the mouth, the roof of the mouth, the poll, and when used with a curb chain, the chin groove.

CURB CHAIN   designed to apply pressure to the chin groove when a rider pulls the curb reins. It is a short metal chain, attached to the bit at the bridle rings, which lies under the horse's chin; it can be used with a curb or a pelham bit. Two fingers should fit between the chain and the horse's jaw when it is attached to the bridle.

DISUNITED   a term used to describe the gait of a horse that is leading its canter with a pair of diagonal legs rather than the correct hind leg.

DROPPED NOSEBAND   a noseband designed to keep a horse from opening its mouth away from the bit; it fits two to three inches above the nostrils. I feel strongly that it should not be used because it does not allow a horse to communicate its fear or displeasure to a rider, and it can be painful.

EWE-NECKED   a term used to describe a neck that in profile has no crest but rather a sagging top and bottom line. It is difficult for horses with this type of neck to flex it properly at the poll, so when asked to stop with the bit, they usually throw their heads up.

GALLOP   a four-beat gait which is similar to the canter except that the paired diagonal legs do not land at the same time. In the left lead, the order of legs striking the ground is as follows: 1. right hind leg; 2. left hind leg; 3. right foreleg; 4. left foreleg. The four beats are followed by a moment of suspension when all four legs are off the ground. In a right lead, the left hind leg begins the sequence.

GLOSTER NOSEBAND   a device designed to retrain a horse that has the wrong head carriage. Used simply as a bitless bridle it applies pressure to a horse's nose, but it can also be used in combination with a neck strap for extra power.

GYMKHANA   a competition based on riders' skill at games on horseback. Some common gymkhana games are figure-8 races, barrel races, and relay races.

HALF-PASSAGE   a diagonal movement forward and sidewise. When the horse is moving in a half-passage to the right, its left foreleg should pass in front of its right foreleg; vice versa if the horse is moving to the left.

HALTER   a piece of tack used for holding, leading, or tying up a horse. It consists of a headpiece, a throatlatch, cheekpieces, and a noseband.

HAND   a measurement used in determining the height of a horse or pony. Four inches make up a hand, and a horse is measured by the number of hands in a straight line from the top of its withers to the bottom of the hoof of its foreleg.

HEAVES   a lung condition characterized by a constant cough, trouble forcing air out of the lungs, and little stamina. Its cause is an allergic reaction, persistent coughing induced by a dusty stall, or dusty hay. Once a horse has the heaves it cannot be cured, but keeping its feed free of dust and mold, keeping its bedding as free of dust as possible, and keeping it at pasture if dust is a problem in the barn are ways to help manage the condition.

HOG or ROACH   a term that describes the process of cutting a mane short. This is usually done for convenience' sake because the owner doesn't have time to care for a long mane.

LAMINITIS or FOUNDER   an inflammation of the laminae of the foot which is very painful. The affected foot will be hot, and a horse with this condition usually stands with its hind feet well up under its body to relieve some of the pressure caused by the inflammation. Laminitis can be caused by many things, including overwork on a hard surface, drinking large amounts of cold water when overheated, and overeating. Some relief can be given to the horse by standing it in cool mud or by wrapping its fetlocks and feet with gunnysacks and running a hose on them. A veterinarian should be called if you suspect this condition.

LUNGEING REIN   a line twenty to thirty feet long used to exercise a horse without riding it or for training. It can be attached to the side ring of an ordinary halter, and a lungeing whip (never used directly on the horse) is used with it to encourage the horse to trot or canter in a circle around the person holding the line.

MARTINGALE   a leather strap designed to keep a horse from carrying its head too high or from throwing its head up. A standing martingale is attached to the noseband; a running martingale, which is not attached to the noseband, has two rings on one end through which the reins are run. Either type of martingale passes through a neck strap and is connected to the girth.

MAIDEN   a mare that has never been bred (or in racing terminology, any horse that has never won a race).

NAVICULAR   an inflammation of the navicular bone in the forefeet. A horse with this condition will usually go lame and point the affected foot when standing. The disease may be caused by overwork, and horses with upright pasterns or small feet are more liable to contract it. Special shoes with raised heels and pads are used to help the horse; they reduce the force of impact to the navicular bone when the horse is working.

NEAR SIDE   the left side of the horse. A rider always mounts and makes adjustments to the girth from this side. A horse is also led from his near side.

NECK REINING   a method of turning a horse by simply laying the rein on the horse's neck opposite the way you wish to turn rather than by pulling on the bit. If you want the horse to go right, move your hand holding both reins to the right; the left rein will thus apply pressure to the left side of the horse's neck, and the horse will move away from it.

OFF SIDE   the right side of a horse.

PASSAGE   a lateral movement of the horse with the left forefoot passing in front of the right forefoot if the horse is moving right. In dressage, or very advanced riding, passage is a collected, elevated trot with a long moment of suspension.

PELHAM   a double-reined bit designed to allow a rider to apply simple snaffle-bit action with one set of reins and curb-bit action with the other set if the horse misbehaves. There are snaffle rings on the mouthpiece, which can be either curb or straight-bar, to which one set of reins is attached. The other set is attached to the loops at the ends of the shanks. Pulling on the set attached to the mouthpiece (the snaffle reins) will apply pressure across the tongue and on the bars of the mouth. Pulling on the set attached to the ends of the shanks (the curb reins) will apply pressure on the poll as well and to the chin groove if the curb chain is in place.

POSTING a smooth, rhythmical up-and-down motion made by a rider when her horse is at the trot. As the horse's diagonal pair of legs leave the ground, the rider pushes herself up out of the saddle and slightly forward. As this same pair of legs strike the ground the rider gently returns to the saddle. The movement is repeated in rhythm with this diagonal pair of legs on a "one-two, one-two" count.

QUEENSLAND ITCH an allergic itchiness caused by small biting gnats. This condition usually occurs in the warmer seasons when the gnats are most prevalent. A horse or pony will rub its coat bare in places in its efforts to relieve the itchiness, and a veterinarian should be consulted.

RINGWORM a disease which can be caused by several types of fungi. Round reddish sores covered with small scales will appear on the skin. A veterinarian should be called, and the spots should not be touched because some types of ringworm can be contracted by people.

ROARER a horse that makes a whistling noise when breathing heavily. If your horse has this condition you will be able to hear the whistle when it breathes in. Roaring can be caused by broken trachea rings or by paralysis of the muscles at the top of the windpipe; these sagging muscles produce the whistle as air rushes through them. In most cases, roaring can be surgically corrected; if not taken care of, it gets progressively worse.

SNAFFLE BIT a simple, mild bit. The mouthpiece is either straight across or jointed in the middle, with rings at either end for the reins. The larger the mouthpiece the less severe the bit, because its pressure is distributed over a larger area.

SPLINTS bony enlargements on a horse's cannon and/or splint bones. They are caused by excessive strain (especially on young horses whose bones have not yet finished growing) or a blow to the affected area. If not treated, the splint will calcify and form a permanent hard lump. Splints do not usually cause lameness except in the early stages.

STANDING STALL an enclosure in a barn where a horse is kept at night or when not in use. It is eight to ten feet long and five to six feet wide. In it a horse is unable to lie down or turn around.

STRANGLES   a disease in which the lymph glands of the horse's throat and jaw swell and fill with pus. It is caused by a bacterial infection, and the symptoms are fever, a runny nose, and difficulty in swallowing. The horse's glands may burst if they become too swollen, and a veterinarian should be called immediately.

SURCINGLE   a belt used to hold the horse's blanket in place. It passes under the belly and is buckled over the blanket on the horse's back.

TACK   the word used for all of a horse's leather equipment.

TRACE CLIP   a partial clip given to provide adequate ventilation for a working horse, as well as protection. It begins under the throat and continues down the chest and under the belly. The legs remain unclipped, but the sides are clipped up to where a harness trace line would be if the horse were hitched to a cart. This is from the days when horses were used to draw all forms of transportation. It is a good clip for a horse at grass, because it leaves the horse with some protection from being cut by brambles.

TROT   a two-beat gait in which a diagonal pair of legs strike the ground simultaneously and alternately with the other diagonal pair of legs. Between each beat and the next there is a moment of suspension when all four legs are off the ground.

WALK   a four-beat gait in which each foot strikes the ground separately. There is no moment of suspension, since at least two feet are always on the ground at the same time. The order in which they strike the ground is as follows: 1. left hind foot; 2. left forefoot; 3. right hind foot; 4. right forefoot.

WIND-PUFFS   swellings of the fluid sacs located around the pastern and fetlock joints on a horse's forefeet and hind feet. They are a result of hard work on hard surfaces or of heavy work for an extended period of time. Usually they are not serious and do not cause lameness.

WIND SUCKING   a vice in which a horse sets its teeth on a post or side of a stall, arches its neck and sucks in large quantities of air. The habit can lead to colic or other digestive problems because of the excessive amount of air brought into the digestive tract. A neck strap placed tightly around the throat often keeps a horse from doing this because when the animal arches its neck the strap puts pressure on the trachea. Another good deterrent is coating all surfaces the horse might use to wind-suck with creosote.

·Index

ABOUT THE AUTHOR

BARBARA WOODHOUSE is known to millions of Americans through the publication of her best-selling book *No Bad Dogs;* her enormously successful television series "Train Your Dog the Woodhouse Way" and her frequent appearances on national television shows such as "60 Minutes," "The Tonight Show" and "Good Morning America." She was born near Dublin in 1910 and raised in Oxford, England. As a young woman she ran a riding school and then spent four years in Argentina on a cattle *estancia.* After a few years, she was given the job of official horse-breaker to the cattle company. She returned to England where she married Dr. Michael Woodhouse, raised a family, ran a farm, broke in horses, bred Arab horses and trained thousands of dogs "The Woodhouse Way."